Rifled Sanctuaries

'A village under heathenism — sun worship', 'The same village, under Christianity.'
From Life in the Southern Isles by William Wyatt Gill (1876).
(Mitchell Library, Sydney photograph)

RIFLED SANCTUARIES

Some Views of the Pacific Islands
in Western Literature to 1900

The Macmillan Brown Lectures 1982

Bill Pearson

AUCKLAND UNIVERSITY PRESS
OXFORD UNIVERSITY PRESS

BY THE SAME AUTHOR
Coal Flat
Henry Lawson among Maoris
Fretful Sleepers and Other Essays

© Bill Pearson 1984
First published 1984
Printed in New Zealand
at the University of Auckland Bindery
ISBN 0 19 648029 9

To Donald Stenhouse

ACKNOWLEDGEMENTS

This book is an expanded version of the Macmillan Brown Lectures for 1982 given at the University of Auckland on 8, 15, and 22 September.

Much of the earlier reading was done during the tenure of a research fellowship in the Research School of Pacific Studies at the Australian National University. There are many concealed debts to colleagues, then or since, in the Department of Pacific and South-East Asian History, notably the late J. W. Davidson, H. E. Maude, Gavan Daws, Niel Gunson, R. M. Langdon, and Dorothy Shineberg. Others whose expertise outside my field has helped are Peter Bellwood, Ross Clark, Jack Golson, Jacques Guy, A. B. Hooper, Hugh Laracy, and Nigel Wace.

For sharing with me his knowledge of Benjamin Morrell I am especially grateful to Henry Stommel of Woods Hole Oceanographic Institution, Massachusetts. Joe Atkinson arranged a copy of a thesis otherwise difficult to obtain. Keith and Judith Sorrenson transcribed from a source at the time inaccessible to me.

To the staff of these libraries I have been indebted: the Mitchell Library and Dixson Collection, State Library of New South Wales; the National Library of Australia; the Australian National University Library; the British Library; New York Public Library; the G. W. Blunt White Library at Mystic, Connecticut; the Essex Institute, Salem, Massachusetts; the Boston Public Library; the Widener Library at Harvard University; the libraries of Brown University, the University of Pennsylvania, and the University of Hawaii.

CONTENTS

Acknowledgements		*7*
1	*Fall from Grace*	*11*
2	*Rescue and Captivity*	*30*
3	*Views from the Beach*	*59*
References		*83*
Index		*89*

1
FALL FROM GRACE

It is an honour to contribute to this series of annual lectures to commemorate the first professor of English at my alma mater, the old Canterbury University College. John Macmillan Brown has several claims on our interest. He was the father of Millicent Baxter, father-in-law of Archibald Baxter, both of whose memoirs have enriched our literature. And he was grandfather to the poet James K. Baxter who once gave the Macmillan Brown lectures himself, and was a friend of and formative influence on the contemporary Pacific writer, Albert Wendt.

Macmillan Brown was professor of English, history, and political economy, and after his retirement in 1895 took an increasing interest in the Pacific. Among his several Pacific works there are two novels, a utopia called *Limanora* and a satirical account of an imaginary island called *Riallaro*. But the genre of the imaginary voyage is one I am excluding from my talks because I am concerned with the reactions of Europeans to the actual people of the Pacific islands, to their behaviour and their cultures, which were so often misunderstood by the early visitors, or treated as illustrations of European preoccupations.

Macmillan Brown's wide-ranging example is appropriate because though I am concerned with literary responses to the Pacific islands, and have read far more imaginative writing than I can mention, I have to recognize that much of it is of slight literary value, and that it has to be considered in its historical context, and that its meaning relates more to the history of European ideas and attitudes than to literature. Because we have to understand these ideas and attitudes as they were actually stated, I hope that Pacific islands people who are present will not be offended at some of the things that have been said. If I feel that I have to quote them, I don't share them.

The period that is seminal is from 1767, when Europe and Tahiti made first reported contact, to the mid-nineteenth century, and much of my first two lectures will be concerned with this time. Much of that literature is mediated and vicarious. In my third lecture I will discuss the writing of those who drew on their own experience of the Pacific, and though I will not be able to discuss it fully or closely I will touch on the recent vigorous literature in English by Pacific island-born writers, whose view of their experience has been a measure of lifelikeness throughout the writing of the lectures.

I begin with one cultural institution whose licentiousness shocked Europe, not because, to many, it seemed to demand the vengeance of Heaven; I do so because it involved dramatic performances. This was the privileged sect in Tahiti called the arioi, ostensibly a set of strolling players, to which so many predominantly upper class young men and a smaller number of women belonged, whose main public activity when they went on circuit was dramatic performance and dancing.[1] There were troupes of players in the Leeward group when Cook made two visits in 1773 and 1774, on his second voyage to the Pacific. They gave a number of performances and we have impressions of them from several of the ship's company.

There was one piece recorded by the German botanist Johann Reinhold Forster. This is its plot. A father won't let his daughter marry but her lover persuades her to run away with him. She is seen on the acting area in labour and gives birth to a son so vigorous that he is played by an adult. He runs about the area with placenta and cord still attached while the midwife tries to catch him. The father, impressed with his grandson's cleverness, is reconciled to his son-in-law.

Another plot must have been popular: it was acted in Huahine, Taha'a and Ra'iatea, as well as Tahiti. It showed some thieves dexterously stealing property in the keeping of sleeping servants. There were variants of this plot; sometimes the thieves were detected, sometimes not. In the version that Cook saw at Ra'iatea, the thieves were discovered but put up a fight and got away. Cook, troubled by repeated thefts wherever he went, watched this play very closely. 'I was very attentive to the whole of this part in expectation that it would have had a quite different end, for I had . . . understood that the Theift was to be punished with death or with a good . . . (beating) but I found my self misstaken in both.'[2]

There is a topical piece on which we have several comments. William Wales, the astronomer, describes it and Johann Reinhold Forster moralizes on it. It was performed at Huahine and concerned a girl who in actuality was in the audience. She came from Porapora and had eloped from there to Tahiti with a young chief, an arioi, who then neglected her. She had joined Cook's ship at Tahiti to get a passage back home to Porapora. Cook describes it: 'The Piece concluded with the reception she was supposed to meet with from her friends at her return which was not a favourable one.' Throughout the performance the girl was in tears and the midshipmen in whose company she was had difficulty persuading her to sit through it. Wales thought it was 'very Cruel', though he speculated that the local people saw it as 'a very wholsome and even Necessary piece of Satire' and noted that it caused a change of mind in two local girls who had agreed to sleep on board.[3] Johann Reinhold Forster drew a number of comforting lessons from the whole performance, both on the acting area and in the audience. The poor girl, he said, had been 'the object of indelicate, but sharp and salutary satire' and the actors had exposed immorality for the instruction of the rising generation even though she was protected by powerful foreigners. The audience had laughed at the actors' sarcasms, but the girl's tears were proof of her repentance; the audience noted that, and came to comfort her and assure her of their friendship; and 'in a manner to thank her for having contributed to the innocent mirth, as well as to the instruction and the warning of her country women'. Forster senior continues: 'We must give the palm to the O-Taheiteans, who, like true children of nature, have a sympathizing tear, and unrestrained feelings, the tribute and glory of humanity, in readiness on all proper occasions.'[4]

I opened with these samples of drama of Polynesians about themselves, partly because the zest and the ridicule look forward to recent Polynesian writing in English, and because I don't find it difficult to visualize similar skits being extemporized and enjoyed by Polynesians I know — it is an aspect of Polynesian behaviour that came to be forgotten by Europeans who concerned themselves with their welfare. But I raised them also because the incident reveals the European compulsion to look for a moral, and in Johann Reinhold Forster's case to expound a complex pattern of moralizing which illustrates, in his mind, a commendable and fashionable sensibility in the islanders. If one were to draw his meaning out a little more finely, they were people with minds rather like his own, and the portrait is to some extent a self-portrait.

It was Tahiti — or the Society Islands as a whole — that made the first benign impact on Europe. If at first it is Tahiti I concentrate on, it is because that was what Europe was most interested in. Reading the accounts of the early visitors, even sceptically, it is fairly plain that Tahitian life at the time of European contact was pleasant in time of peace, and had many satisfactions and delights for most of the people. It is difficult not to agree with the finding of Johann Reinhold's son Georg Forster, that 'allowing for the imperfect state of sublunary happiness, which is comparative at best, there are not, I believe, many nations existing whose situation is so desirable.'[5] At the same time it is apparent, in the light of what has been learned subsequently about ancient Tahitian society, that the terms in which Europe judged it, and by which it came to destroy it, were inadequate to understanding it in the way that Tahitians must have understood themselves.

Let us briefly rehearse these early visits and reports.[6] It was the English captain Samuel Wallis who first visited Tahiti, in 1767. There was resistance to English attempts to land, and Wallis's ship was attacked; eventually the English destroyed the Tahitian fleet and the people were shocked at the unfamiliar destructive power of English weapons. Thereafter for several weeks there were amicable relations in which sailors took pleasure in the sexual freedom allowed to girls between puberty and marriage, and Tahitians on their side sought the new material iron. A district chief's wife, Purea, for purposes not apparent, cultivated the friendship of the English and wept copiously at their departure. Such weeping can be seen from other instances to be a ceremonial honour awarded to guests who were welcome. Nine months later the French captain Louis Antoine de Bougainville called, unaware of the English visit, and, though he found his welcome uncertain, since he was not allowed to land except by day or to stay as long as he first asked, his crew were generously entertained by the young girls, and he was intrigued and moved to rhapsodic prose by the absence of shame or secrecy in their embraces. He composed a pastoral idyll, using the metaphor of the isle of Cythera, home of Venus, every inhabitant a servant of love; and saw Tahitians as living in the Golden Age, without war, or private property. Their bread grew on trees; they lived an enviably simple life on a frugal diet of fruit and fish and coconut milk. It was an attractive portrait, one that flattered its readers, as well as its author.

It is not, as has been often loosely said, identical with the happy stage of human development that Rousseau hypothesized in his *Discourse on the Origins of Inequality*, the stage before humankind had metals and agriculture, from which developed private property and its attendant passions of luxury, greed, envy, and ambition. A feature of Rousseau's happy stage — which, of course, was irrecoverable for those societies that had passed it — was an active life and a frugal diet. Bougainville's picture emphasizes the indolence of a people whose bread grew on trees, whose fruit grew without cultivation, and indolence is an obvious source of luxury and loss of happiness. Cook was to object in the journal of his second voyage that there was in fact private property in Tahiti, that all fruits require labour, and even breadfruit and coconuts, let alone plantains and bananas, need proper cultivation. But that was not published until six years later and in any case had to compete with a statement attributed to Cook in Hawkesworth's account of his first voyage, a statement that in fact had been made by Banks (but, as Cook's journal shows, broadly accepted by Cook at that time). This calculated that, in contrast with the repeated and laborious sowings and reapings required for European crops, no more than an hour's labour in planting ten breadfruit trees will supply the needs of a family through several generations.[7] The view of bountiful nature and indolent inhabitants prevailed. Even before Bougainville had published, there was talk in Paris about the Tahitian that he had brought with him, Ahutoru, and one writer used the happiness of Tahitians to confute Rousseau.[8]

But Bougainville's picture was no more sincere than most gallant compliments are. It has to be measured against the historical actuality of Bougainville's instructions to his crew that thieves were to be shot at, and the four Tahitian casualties that followed trading disputes in the nine days of the French stay. And there are flaws in the portrait; the attitudes of settlers and traders of a century later are incipient. The Tahitians are alert but fickle; they can't keep their minds on anything for two minutes on end; they are lazy-minded, and if their wants are few so are their ideas.[9] If that is not enough to undermine Bougainville's credit as the primitivist he has been represented to be, there are his remarks to his friend Gudin de la Brenellerie that the happiest people were in fact Europeans, that South Sea Islanders were not to be envied because they had no metals, were constantly at war, were bold and greedy thieves, and because of the uncertainty of their subsistence relied on cannibalism. (It is not clear if he excepted Tahitians from this judgement, but of them he said that their easy life had hindered their development.)[10]

If these remarks on South Sea islanders did represent a change of view rather than the confession of a previously withheld one, it was a change that many people can be seen to make in the late eighteenth century, gradually or rapidly: the earlier benignity was no more profound than a passing mood. Bougainville's experience of Melanesia was not so enchanting — there was bloodshed off Choiseul — but that had not been sufficient to cause him to revise his euphoric view of Tahiti. Nor did he go back to the Pacific. The change (if it was a change) could only have been brought about by reading, and the only report to appear between the publication of Bougainville's own book and that of his friend, was John Hawkesworth's edition of the four voyages of Wallis, John Byron, Carteret and Cook. Cook's visit in 1769 is well known; he found the Tahitians very co-operative and attributed it to Wallis's bombardment. It used to be said that Hawkesworth sentimentalized the journals he edited, idealizing the Polynesians. In fact, a collation of his book with the texts of the logs and journals he used shows the reverse to be true.[11] He is the first implanter of the malign attitudes that dominated the nineteenth century. I have written about Hawkesworth's editorial strategies before, but it is necessary to repeat one or two of their features. He overvalued himself as a philosopher, and he felt a challenge to improve on his sources with suitable moral conclusions not apparent to sea-captains. He wrote the four voyages as a first-person narrative as if it were the same commander — or four commanders of like outlook — reflecting on all this experience, and he incorporated observations from supplementary journals, notably those of George Robertson the master of Wallis's ship the *Dolphin*, and Joseph Banks the botanist on Cook's first voyage. He ignored the ship's master's humane and commonsense judgements that the Tahitians were a 'Smart Sensable people' with 'Fine Young Girls' and 'fine brisk-spirited women', and preferred to see them in terms of the philosophical question of whether or not their way of life was a matter for European envy. He invents a number of comic incidents for which the journals give no authority, all turning on the technological superiority of the English: he presents the Tahitians as children, fickle in mood and attention, with little reflection or forethought. There are recurring tilts at those who advocate primitivist simplicity, and he concludes that if we admit that Tahitians are happier than we, then we have to admit that the child is happier than the man, and the adult a loser by his education — which for Hawkesworth in 1773 was self-evidently nonsense.

There is an incident where Hawkesworth uses Banks to criticize Cook. In retaliation for some thefts, Cook had impounded some canoes filled with catches of fish; and at a certain point Banks expressed, in his journal, doubts as to the wisdom of his policy. Cook's policy in fact did not achieve the results he looked for. So Hawkesworth, wishing to underline the failure, turns Banks's doubts into Cook's reflections after the event. On another occasion where an inhabitant was shot for making off with a musket, Cook was uneasy about the shooting, but Hawkesworth leaves the reader confident that the local people have accepted the explanation that Banks gave them. When Cook arrested the high chiefs as hostages against the return of two deserters, they were justifiably resentful since he was indebted to them for assistance and hospitality. When they were released, they presented him with four hogs for which they would take no payment. Cook recognized the gesture as a reproach and was embarrassed; he didn't accept the gift. But Hawkesworth turns the incident into an expression of gratitude for Cook's leniency, and on Cook's part a moral firmness about fair payment: an incident that seals an increased mutual respect, and leaves Cook in a position of moral advantage.

What is emerging is a first outline of that figure of late nineteenth-century boys' adventure fiction, the consciously magnanimous British commander, and what is implied is a colonial relationship, a prudent handling of a people under tutelage, grateful and tractable. At best the Tahitians are treated with patronizing indulgence — 'these people', 'our Indian friends' — but their thefts and their sexual incontinence could not be countenanced. They were 'the errantest thieves upon the face of the earth' (a judgement more severe than its source in Banks) and Hawkesworth could not mention without disapproval the dedicated promiscuity of the arioi and the obligatory killing of any babies born as a result. In an arch style that shocked reviewers Hawkesworth told the incident, so cool-headedly described by Cook, in which an arioi made love to a twelve-year-old, in witness of a small crowd that included Purea, who called out advice to the girl. These people, he said, had ascended 'a scale in dissolute sensuality' beyond imagination and unknown in any society whose habits had ever been recorded. This is not the innocent child of nature, but the depraved savage.

Hawkesworth's *Voyages* was published in 1773; its three volumes were widely read in Britain, though educated men like Samuel Johnson, Horace Walpole, and the Forsters dismissed the book as trivial. Charles Wesley could not believe that people could couple in public. Within a year Hawkesworth had gone into a second edition and been translated into three European languages; he was pirated in New York and Dublin. For a hundred and twenty years, well after his name was forgotten, his words had currency, verbatim or in paraphrase, in dozens of lives of Cook, collections of voyages, editions or translations of Cook, and retellings for children.

Cook's journal of his second voyage, more scrupulously edited by John Douglas, corrected some of the wilder statements about the promiscuity of Tahitian women, but that was published four years after Hawkesworth. However, the main literary reaction to Hawkesworth was as trivial as the several learned men thought the book itself to be. There were thirteen satirical poems, six of them published within a year, most of them before the end of 1780. It is tempting to quote them because they are impudent and obscene; but they have been extensively treated by Bernard Smith, E. H. McCormick, and Colin Roderick, and I will pass over them briefly.[12] These lampoons concentrate on five incidents reported by Hawkesworth that lend themselves to the ridicule of Banks or to the slander of the chief's wife, Purea, under the name Oberea, presenting her as thief and adulteress, a painted whore, 'savage slut', 'wanton Gipsy', 'dirty Queen'. They dwell on her 'painted breech', her 'tattowed bum'. There is an emphasis on physical detail that reflects an extremely puritanical disgust with the flesh: in one poem a Tahitian is mocked trying to play the noseflute as he sounds a lament for the nose he has lost from syphilis. If the tone is disgust, the purpose is hysterically moral. In one lampoon by Peter Pindar, Decency, personified, is so angry at the demonstrations of Tahitian dancing at Banks's seat at Hinchingbrook that

> *She*, blushing damsel, turn'd her head aside
> And wish'd a whip to ev'ry hopping hide.[13]

One anonymous poem, still in the same uninventive heroic couplets, confines its satire to Britain, where Ma'i the Ra'iatean Cook brought with him who was known in Britain as Omai (the subject of E. H. McCormick's thorough research), adopts the posture of critical visitor from the East, and consequently criticizes English vices from the position of the inhabitant of a country free from depravity, interest, fashion, or prejudice. English follies and English hypocrisy are the object of this satire and, in relation to this, the poet praises the simplicity and candour that justify Tahitian unrestraint:

> Raptures repeated on delights should rise,
> Bloom o'er the cheeks, and languish in the eyes,
> Thus might we long indulge extatic flames,
> And leave chill virtue to *European* dames.

Omai wishes

> To taste beneath some plantain's friendly shade,
> The warm endearments of a willing maid, . . .
> . . . . . .
> Taste unrestrain'd what Freedom really means:
> And glow inspir'd with that enthusiast zeal,
> Which *Britons* talk of, *Otaheiteans* feel.[14]

I suspect that this poem is dryly sending up the myth of the zealous lovers of Tahiti at the same time as it more openly lampoons English pretence at virtue. However that may be, it is this poem and its ostensible attitudes that are satirized thirteen years later, in the year of the French Revolution, in a poem by the Tory John Hookham Frere who combined with George Canning the Whig turned Tory, to found a weekly paper, the *Anti-Jacobin*.

> Learn hence, each nymph, whose free aspiring mind
> Europe's cold laws, and colder customs bind —
> O! learn, what Nature's genial laws decree —
> What Otaheite is, let Britain be! [15]

The poem pretends to be an argument against marriage. So Frere staves off the threat that the championship of a loose morality presents to English society. It is notable that, now, defence of Tahiti is classed with revolution, but the authors of the earlier satires were men of both Whig and Tory sentiment, men who were to become both supporters and opponents of the French Revolution. Another satire, never published, was attempted by the twelve-year-old budding poet, Robert Southey, a satire on English manners 'as delivered by Omai, the Taheitean, to his countrymen on return'.[16] Southey, as Byron and Hazlitt liked to remind him in later years, had his Jacobin phase before he became a supporter of legitimacy and, I should add, a deplorer of Tahitian manners.

Of the early accounts of Pacific island societies, only those of the Forsters, father and son, can be described as genuinely primitivist — moved by a desire to present pre-literate societies as favoured. The Forsters were naturalists on Cook's second voyage, and both of them helped to write the lengthy account of the voyage published over the name of George Forster who was only twenty-one when he returned to England. The father, Johann Reinhold, compiled his more systematic

Observations. Both books were translated into German and French and were more influential on the Continent than in England. In Tahiti George Forster found 'convincing proof of the excellence of the human heart, in its simple state, before ambition, luxury, and various other passions have corrupted it'.[17] Though Forster in one place dissociates himself from Rousseau, there is clearly an echo of Rousseau's second Discourse here, or at least of ideas that Rousseau shared with others of the time. The Forsters saw Tahitian life in the way that some eighteenth-century thinkers had seen American Indian life, as something like the happy stage of simplicity that mankind had once enjoyed, when people lived in small groups, when family affections were simple and strong, diet was frugal, and property was held in common. But George Forster found defects. When he saw a corpulent chief being hand-fed, he detected luxury; when a district chief invited Cook to stay longer but hesitated when he found what it would cost him in supplying provisions, Forster detected courtly hypocrisy. Yet Tahitian society met the essential criterion of happiness: the people's economic needs were easily satisfied since their wants were few and they weren't aware of any others. For their happiness to continue it was important that they should not learn other needs. George Forster expressed a wish that he must have known was contrary to the likely outcome of the voyage in which he was participating, a wish that contact with Europeans could be 'broken off in time, before a corruption of manners which unhappily characterizes civilized regions, may reach that innocent race of men, who live here fortunate in their ignorance and simplicity'. Forster then comments on his wish: 'But it is a melancholy truth, that the dictates of philanthropy do not harmonize with the political systems of Europe!'[18] In that concession, is he not resigning his admired 'children of nature' to a less admirable historical destiny? Isn't he deploring in advance the acculturated Polynesian? It is notable that Johann Reinhold Forster's schema of the four stages of development of human society — a common model at the time — puts Tahitians at the top of the stage of Savagery which is metaphorically described as childhood.[19] 'Children of nature' in a stage likened to childhood: an attitude not colonialist in tendency, but paternalist. The older Forster's model is of developmental progression and it assumes that societies could be evaluated and ordered into gradations of superiority. Such gradations carried racist implications. Australians and the Indians of Tierra del Fuego were at the bottom of the scale in the stage of Animality, Europeans were at the top, in the stage of

Civilization. In the Pacific, the Forsters favoured Polynesians more than Melanesians. In Malekula they likened the people to monkeys. But the deepest objection to the attitudes that underlie the *Observations* is that its author assumes that the terms philosophers like himself could bring to Pacific cultures were sufficient to understand them.

It is possible to see the attitude of the Forsters as comparable in structure to those of the missionaries of thirty years later. The sets of participants are good or bad. They disapprove of the common sailor, coarse, randy and trigger-happy; they disapprove in advance of the corrupted Polynesian; the approved Tahitian is the unspoiled Tahitian of the present, and the approved European is the philanthropist like the Forsters themselves. Replace the philanthropist with the messengers of grace, and it is only a rearrangement of oppositions — an over-simplified view that was to dominate the vicarious literature of the first half of the nineteenth century.

There is a vignette in George Forster, of a three-generation family group resting after a frugal meal. A venerable old man with silvery locks and beard lies on a mat while his grandchildren play around him. He invites the visitors to sit; he offers them drinks of coconut milk and fruit juice: they ask one another's names, a young man entertains them with a song while another accompanies him on a nose-flute. There is another passage which describes the daily round of the ordinary middle class Tahitian: I have met it, lifted in full without attribution, in two of the French imaginative works I have read. It ends with the evening's pursuits: 'the lively jest, without any ill-nature, the artless tale, the jocund dance and frugal supper, bring on the evening; and another visit to the river concludes the actions of the day. Thus contented with their simple way of life, and placed in a delightful country, they are free from cares, and happy in their ignorance.' [20]

It must have been passages like these that moved the professor of Hebrew at Trinity College Dublin to lament the corruption of this enclave of innocence in a poem titled *The Injured Islanders* published in 1779. When Cook went to Tahiti the first time he found that the fortunes of Wallis's hostess Purea had suffered a reversal and that she and her husband, Amo, had been defeated in an inter-clan war. Over a century later Henry Adams was to learn the reason from the traditions of the Teva clan, to which Amo had belonged. The chiefs of other clans were outraged at Purea's presumptuous promotion of the political claims of her infant son Teri'irere, and had joined forces to resist them.[21] Purea's loss of power was reported in Hawkesworth, but the Rev Gerald Fitzgerald, the Dublin professor, had then been unmoved because he found Hawkesworth's Tahitians 'fitter subjects for Ridicule than Panegyrick'. It was Forster who inspired this poem written in the metre and the diction of Goldsmith's *The Deserted Village*, and imbued with its mood. The poem takes the form of an elegy spoken by Oberea, rhetorically addressed to Wallis. The lost innocence is seen in terms of that eighteenth-century nostalgia for the small, plain-living community, the three-generation family bound by filial piety:

> Ah! What a Change from all that charm'd before,
> When kindred Love connected ev'ry Shore,
> When mutual Interest, spreading unconfin'd,
> Parental Care and Filial Duty join'd —
> Such were the Bands that held our happy State,
> Ere Lux'ry taught Ambition to be great —
> Ere Lust of Power to Deeds oppressive led —
> Ere Europe's Crimes with Europe's Commerce spread. . . .[22]

Though in fact it is Wallis who brought the damage, Oberea appeals to him to return to repair it, unable to do anything herself, it seems. She stands in a literary posture of unrequited love, as Dido to Aeneas, vainly watching the shore for his return. In fact this literary posture is a distraction from the problem presented, which is not specified so clearly in the poem as in a prose preface in which Fitzgerald balances the commercial and scientific advantages of the voyages of discovery against the injuries done to the inhabitants. The poem can only be seen as a posture, known to be ineffective, like Oberea's own, watching for the ship that will never come; in fact little more than a European gesture of conscience, expressed in an imitative form.

Most of the literary treatment of the Pacific was in terms of already established cliches of form and diction, to point some occasional moral or other. To take some French examples: sympathetic though they are, they depict Tahitians in terms of French literary conventions currently in fashion. Mme de Monbart writes a touching epistolary romance, *Lettres Taitiennes*, in which a Tahitian with the exotic name of Zeïr fulfils several familiar roles: he is the critical visitor from the East, the man of sentiment, the hero of sentimental romances. He discovers that French women are no less keen on love than Tahitians, but learns that they value secrecy, and his first love repairs to a convent when their affair is exposed, though her husband becomes Zeïr's best friend. Zeïr passes through two affairs, one of them ending in death. His lover back home, Zulica, writes to him. Zeïr is seduced by his easy conquests of duchesses at Versailles, and is trapped by his own rash promise to a possessive intellectual woman who is jealous of Zulica and persuades him to marry her before she dies. Zulica in the meantime has come to France and in the end she and Zeïr marry, with the blessing of his former lover, the nun, whom he continues to love in his heart (in second place) with his wife's blessing — a solution that not only preserves the laws of love and honour, and the double standard of fidelity for men and for women, but avoids a racially mixed marriage that lasts longer than a few days.[23] Impermanence is a feature of most of the mixed love affairs in writing about the Pacific.

But for the most part Tahiti was the occasion for expounding social theories or criticisms of French society: Tahiti, for example, as showing the superiority of a morality based not on religion but on nature, or the superiority of a religion whose rites are erotic, or Tahiti as showing the artificiality of French institutions.[24] There are two political projections. One of them goes backward and presents Tahiti as the end-product of a cycle of social upheavals and conquests which began with a Golden Age that was corrupted by the slaughter of animals, and was succeeded by other kinds of society, the second last of which is like contemporary France. This is really another version of the eighteenth-century French imaginary voyage in which a number of kinds of society are visited and judged, and the message is in terms of contemporary thinking about society. This one is notable, however, in two ways: the simple survivors of the earliest society are colonized by civilized neighbours who introduce new economic wants and reduce the local people to poverty. Eventually they conquer another invader, fall into civil war, and are conquered by a Tahitian king, who, in the light of past mistakes, devises a new constitution, under a limited monarchy, with a simple spartan way of life, which is essentially the same as George Forster's description of Tahiti, only the primitivism is hard.[25]

The other political projection was published in the year following the French Revolution and is written by the Abbé Baston, who foresees a future of Tahiti under the direction of the man taken by Cook to England and known as Omai. It is not possible here to do justice to the four volumes of this work, only to follow its political direction. It is based on a reading of the three voyages of Cook. Omai, who voices his sentiments in the rhetoric of heroic drama, becomes an elected chief, abolishes human sacrifice and certain tapu which seemed to have no basis in reason, institutes a number of reforms consistent with revolutionary thinking, and is generalissimo of a revolutionary army. He acts as redresser of wrongs, reliever of the distressed, a king-maker who unites the islands into a political confederation, under a limited monarchy, with a model parliament of two chambers which institutes an enlightened and more puritan constitution. Omai suppresses the arioi. He evicts a European colony which has come to settle, predicting that European settlement means servitude. Finally he introduces Christianity.[26] What he has established is a bourgeois Christian state. And apart from the fact that it is established on the initiative of a Tahitian who himself learned from Europe, the book has points in common with the propagandist writing of English missionaries and their supporters in the nineteenth century.

There is a touching story inset in the Abbé Baston's *Narrations d'Omaï*. It concerns an altruistic noble and his love for a lower-class girl who piously tends her aged and infirm parents. There is an obstacle to their marriage, however, which leads to the temporary disappearance of the girl; and that is that he is an 'arreoy' and any children born to them will have to be killed. Neither is prepared, for one reason or another, to accept a union other than customary marriage. It is not the only occasion where a cultural institution is castigated because it hinders a happy ending for a pair of lovers, usually in terms of bourgeois marriage.

The other important French work inspired by these voyages, though not published for twenty years or so, was Diderot's 'Supplement to Bougainville's Voyage'. Diderot, who sees Tahiti as a society with property held in common, without artificial needs, with a morality based on nature, is aware of its vulnerability now that it had been found by Europe. An old man makes a dire prediction that speaks across the darkness of the nineteenth century to the writing of modern Polynesians — those, at least, who detect in the modern Pacific Islander's mind a regrettable spiritual legacy of colonialism:

> 'One day they will return, in one hand the piece of wood you now see attached to [this man's] belt,* and the other grasping the blade you now see hanging from the belt of another. And with these they will enslave you, murder you or subject you to their extravagances and vices. One day you will serve under them, as corrupted, as vile, as loathsome as themselves.'[27]

* The priest's crucifix.

It is time to recall that all these early reports seeded a ground already prepared by another book, more widely read than any of them, that had been available for fifty years and read in several European languages. Several reviewers in fact referred to it. I mean *Robinson Crusoe*, the only book, by the way, that Rousseau would allow his model pupil Emile to read. It contains a myth of race relations.

We know that Defoe based his narrative on the experience of Alexander Selkirk, marooned at his own request for four years on a Pacific island with no company but his cats and goats, with whom he danced, and that he almost lost the ability to speak his language. Defoe's story of Crusoe on an island off the Orinoco River in Brazil involves other human beings. Two things are notable. The savages that Crusoe never sees at close hand are, and from the first are assumed to be, cannibals. Second is the myth of permanent colonial tutelage that Defoe invents. Crusoe dreams of getting a servant by rescuing a savage when others are pursuing him. In fact he does, killing the pursuers from such a distance that the man whose life he saves is overawed, and so grateful that he kneels and puts Crusoe's foot on his head, not once but twice. Crusoe does not ask his name but gives him one, in terms of his own obsession with time-keeping. He gives him clothes to wear, instructs him in elementary Christian truths, and notes that 'his very affections are ty'd to me, like those of a child to a father'. From now on Friday has no independent existence, no passions, no sex life, no emotional relation to anyone else except his old father who becomes Crusoe's second 'subject'. Crusoe meditates that God has seen fit to offer Friday the occasion of making better use of his human powers as his servant than had been allowed him before, so that he is better off as a servant than when he was free, and that Friday is 'ready, nay more than ready' to so exert those powers. This he calls his 'simple, unfeigned honesty'. Friday is exceptional among savages in stature and handsomeness of countenance; he has straight hair and a pleasant tawny skin colour and an engaging smile. These features of course reflect European criteria of attractiveness.

Now many of the qualities of Friday can be recognized in the mutual responses of Europeans and Polynesians. The benevolence of the Tahitians that Bougainville idyllized was seen very differently by Banks and Cook. When the first Tahitian to greet them crept forward on hands and knees, Banks saw it as entirely due to the awe in which they were held after the astonishing defeat of the Tahitian fleet by the big guns and grape shot of Wallis's *Dolphin* in 1767. Good relations through those ten years of repeated European visits were based on Tahitian recognition of the superiority of European fire-power. Tahitians, Tongans, and Marquesans were praised as being sometimes no darker than Spaniards, attractive in features, models of statuary, intelligent, speculative.

There is one other aspect of Defoe's myth of permanent tutelage. Crusoe enlists Friday to fight other savages and those savages believe that the man who is able to kill from a distance is superhuman. When he leaves the island he takes Friday with him, who does not question his right to do so.

From the many reactions to the death of Cook at Kealakekua Bay on Hawaii in 1777, there are three pieces I am tempted to cite. The first is an elegy by Anna Seward that appeared in 1780 and envisages the conventional elegiac procession of mourners and personified abstractions with emblematic accompaniments, such as the goddesses Flora and Fauna whom Cook has served — Fauna accompanied by a leaping kangaroo and a singing tui and shielded from the sun by a giant bat. But Oberea is there too, given the dignity of her elegiac role, wound up, as it were, to perform her frenzies as maenad,

> Come, Oberea, hapless fair-one! come,
> With piercing shrieks bewail thy Hero's doom! —
> She comes! — she gazes round with dire survey! —
> Oh! fly the mourner on her frantic way.
> See! see! the pointed ivory wounds that head,
> Where late the Loves impurpled roses spread;
> Now stain'd with gore, her raven-tresses flow,
> In ruthless negligence of mad'ning woe;
> Loud she laments! and long the Nymph shall stray
> With wild unequal step round Cook's Morai! [28]

Less respectful to its sources was a pantomime performed in Paris in the year before the French revolution.[29] It was adapted and played in the following year in London, Hull and Dublin. In this Cook is a chivalric intercessor who came to the aid of the King of Hawaii to defeat a rebel, was generous in victory, but was killed by the very man whose life he had spared. The cause of the traitor's rebellion was no more than jealousy in love, and Cook is seen as a supporter of legitimacy whose aid is needed and welcome. It is a pattern that runs through most of the boys' adventure fiction of the late nineteenth century; the magnanimous commander, unwisely lenient, and the ungrateful savage. But in this piece the treacherous savages are in a minority. The approved Hawaiians solemnly mourn like men of proper sensibility, though when the pantomime depicts Hawaiian religious ceremony it is farcical or pretentious.

A malign reaction to the killing of Cook came from the Hull poet Charlotte Beverley:

> Descend Nemesis! and in wrath divine,
> Punish the horrid wretches for their crime;
> Roll! thunders roll! and skies upon them pour
> The greatest plagues that vengeance has in store. . . .[30]

The curse one might see as prophetic since by the end of the century there were few advocates of Tahiti. Cook witnessed a human sacrifice on his last voyage, Bligh described the institutionalized transvestites called *mahu*. By the mid-nineteenth century what seemed an overwhelming case for the prosecution had been built up from several books, particularly three of them, that were frequently cited — cannibalized one could say — to show that Pacific islanders far and wide practised human sacrifice, cannibalism, infanticide, sexual licence, cruelty, sorcery, and superstition. The first of these books was James Wilson's account of the voyage of the *Duff*, which conveyed the first missionaries to Tahiti, Tongatapu, and Tahuata in the Marquesas in 1798. The second was William Ellis's *Polynesian Researches*, published in 1829, enlarged in 1831, boasting of the success of the American mission in Hawaii, and, after a disheartening night of toil, of the London Missionary Society's efforts in the Society Islands. There were further accounts of missionary success on other island groups published in the next ten years or so — John Williams in Melanesia, Samoa, Niue, and the Cook Islands, the Rev. M. Russell's history of missions on the Marquesas, Fiji, Vanuatu, and the Solomons. And in 1845 the report of the United States Exploring Expedition commanded by Charles Wilkes included the account of a three-month visit to Fiji. His informants were whites — missionaries, a beachcomber, a Levuka trader; but the picture, which fuelled missionary tracts and boys' adventure fiction for sixty years, was one of atrocities worse than had been said of Tahiti: cannibalism indulged in for the pleasure of it, extreme cruelty in war, the live burial of widows, the putting to death of the aged, the launching of canoes on the corpses of slaves and using slaves as foundations for the posts of chiefs' new houses. These are practices not to be questioned; but they were judged in simple moralist terms, and the impression was spread that they were every-day events, that every Fijian commoner lived in constant fear of the capricious cruelty of the chiefs, and of being killed for food, and that women lived in terrified subjection. It was with the information provided by these sources that the imagination of writers worked.

In Wilson's account of the voyage of the *Duff*, he graded the islanders he was familiar with in terms of their ripeness for conversion, and if Tahitians came off worst it was because certain practices on the Marquesas had not yet been revealed. The arioi were now presented not only as baby-killers but unwelcome squanderers of the people's food. Wilson found Tahuata in a time of scarcity, the islanders begging for food. But he saw such scarcity as the result of indolence or at least lack of prudence, and he repeated the myth that Europe seemed to need, that food in the islands grew without labour. (In fact Europe might have been surprised if it had heard five years later of a famine from a failure of the breadfruit crop, during which Robarts the beachcomber saw hundreds dying.) Though Wilson found the Tahitians the pleasantest of all islanders in his dealings with them, he judged them the most dissolute, the arioi 'the sink of lewdness and cruelty' and the females 'in the most abject subjection'.[31]

A most notable slanderer of the islanders for thirty years was the some-time poet laureate Robert Southey, who reviewed missionary and travel publications for the *Quarterly Review*, the Tory literary journal founded by those who had started the *Anti-Jacobin*. Southey in his youth had sympathized with the *Bounty* mutineers, and he saw Tahiti as a place where a philosopher might settle 'to introduce the advantages and yet avoid the vices of cultivated society'.[32] Later he urged that the English should colonize Tahiti in order to outnumber the people and as a centre for the anglicization of all Polynesia.[33]

Southey engaged on a lengthy *History of Brazil* (1810-19) in which he sympathetically examined the Jesuit settlements for Indians in Paraguay where the converted Indians had been isolated from demoralizing contact with Spanish soldiers and settlers. In his long poem *A Tale of Paraguay* one sees that for Southey the ideal posture for the converted Indian is trusting submissiveness, and a willingness to die with pious resignation. But Southey's concern for the conversion of Pacific peoples was not to save them from the evils of Europe but from their own. Degeneracy was the lot of fallen man and there was, as Hawkesworth and Wilson had said, no people more degenerate than the Tahitians. Southey was aware of the reproach to Europe that lay in the devastation of South American Indians by the Spanish occupation, but he thought Spanish conduct extenuated by the wickedness exhibited by pagan man in Tahiti.[34] The reason for the excess of it was plain: it was the exemption of the Tahitian from the need to work.[35] In 1803, a couple of months after visiting Samuel Taylor Coleridge at Keswick, he quoted Coleridge's plan 'to mend them by extirpating the bread-fruit from their island, and making them live by the sweat of their brows'.[36] It is ironic that twenty-seven years later when Southey reviewed William Ellis's *Polynesian Researches* he regretted that the Calvinist missionaries had not only made the Tahitians unnecessarily dour, but so meek as to be vulnerable to the possibility of raids from the wild heathens of other Pacific islands, and he urged that the missionaries give them military training.[37]

2
RESCUE AND CAPTIVITY

The imaginative writing in England that drew on the missionary sources I have mentioned was of course vicarious. It was crudely didactic, with repeated citations of the self-evidently shocking institutions of pre-literate peoples, often misunderstood. The dominant theme is the contrast between the disorder and uncertainty of heathen life and the contented order of the meek Christian community, depicted in terms of a rural English village in which the missionary took on the role of village parson and teacher combined, and sometimes adviser to the chief. William Mackword Praed won a university medal for the poem that included this saintly picture of the missionary: the stylistic echoes are still of Goldsmith:

> With furrowed brow and cheek serenely fair,
> The calm wind wandering o'er his silver hair,
> His arm uplifted, and his moistened eye
> Fixed in deep rapture on the golden sky —
> Upon the shore, through many a billow driven,
> He kneels at last, the Messenger of Heaven!
> . . . . . .
> In peace and power he holds his onward path,
> Curbs the fierce soul, and sheathes the murderous steel,
> And calms the passions he hath ceased to feel.[1]

And Robert Grant imagines a missionary on the crater of Kilauea:

> Truth on his lips, and mildness in his eye,
> He looks, he is, a legate from the sky.[2]

On the summit of a more familiar mountain, Skiddaw, James Montgomery contemplated the 'circumnavigation of charity' about to be made by the missionaries George Bennet and Daniel Tyerman; after the voyage he told Bennet that he was 'the most privileged of all that *have* lived or that *do* live, having alone done what never was before attempted'.[3]

The missionary's heroism was enhanced by the ferocity of the people he was to rescue from the captivity of Satan. Since supporters of missions were informed of their activities through the occasional periodical *Missionary Sketches*, containing reports from missions throughout the world, it is to be expected that pre-Christian practices of one Pacific island group were often assumed to be those of other islands; but more than that, Polynesians were accused of practices that belonged to some part of Africa or Asia. Probably such distinctions would have seemed trivial to the readers of the periodical. The savage mind was conceived of as a type, with its various local manifestations. It became a target of ridicule in a book written for a popular market and perhaps for children, published in 1863 and 1864, *Curiosities of Savage Life* by James Greenwood; entertaining, informative, and bolstering a sense of racial privilege.[4] The sources of the book include missionary reports from the Pacific.

Montgomery's picture of the heathen savage has to stand for many. That it is set on Kangaroo Island off the coast of South Australia only indicates the poet's rudimentary sense of geography.

> I saw him sunk in loathsome degradation,
> A naked, fierce, ungovernable savage,
> Companion to the brutes, himself more brutal;
> Superior only in the craft that made
> The serpent subtlest beast of all the field. . . .

Terrible in anger, he danced in his revels to a rumpus of voices, drums and gongs and horns, reaching a degree of hysteria only matched by the tone of the verse that describes it.

> But their prime glory was insane debauch,
> To inflict and bear excruciating tortures;
> The unshrinking victim, while his flesh was rent
> From his live limbs, and eaten in his presence,
> Still in his death-pangs taunted his tormentors
> With tales of cruelty more diabolic,
> Wreak'd by himself upon the friends of those
> Who now their impotence of vengeance wasted
> On him. . . .[5]

In John Dunlop's drama of which I will say more later two 'areoi' in fantastic ornaments dance around the altar, scarifying themselves, provoking the people to a frenzy with cymbals and conch-shells. The King comes on in a red-feather robe and a tiara made of the skulls of defeated enemies, each one wrapped in a coconut leaf. Skulls in fact were always taken to be spoils of war or cannibal feasts. The idea is not entertained that skulls kept on rafters of houses might be the revered relics of ancestors.

A frequent charge was that without Christianity South Sea islanders were lacking in ordinary human affection, and that the desirable small community held together by filial piety is a blessing conferred by Europe. This is celebrated in repeated vignettes like the mother bending over her sleeping babe, a grandparent smiling at the lispings of a grandchild, or the contented intimacy of husband and wife — hallowed joys which were unknown before the message of grace. And the missionaries, it was claimed, brought a new dignity to women. In another university prize poem Samuel Lucas wrote of Hawaii:

> No social bliss could cheer life's dreary span,
> For woman was the powerless slave of man.[6]

Sarah Stickney had married William Ellis, now returned from Tahiti and become secretary of the Missionary Society. She felt keenly the importance of women in civilizing the men. She had written a handbook of gentility for lower-class Englishwomen titled *The Women of England*, in which she urged on them the role of exemplar of the softer virtues. The comfort of a family life was what the heathen lacked.

> No trust in man — perchance in woman less;
> No household loves to soothe him, or to bless;
> . . . . . .
> No joys to make the burdened bosom glad,
> No friendships formed with men of equal mind,
> No woman's converse, social, pure and kind.[7]

The obsession with cannibalism is ambiguous. The point was often made — in a somewhat uneasy tone of triumph at having anticipated all defences — that it was not for sacramental reasons or for revenge that the flesh of enemies was eaten, but for pleasure, and one wasn't safe even from one's family. It seems likely that Europeans wanted to believe that South Sea islanders enjoyed cannibalism because they were repelled and attracted by the idea of cannibalism themselves. The statements quoted were contemporaneous with a zestful piece of popular literature sold in penny weekly numbers in England in 1840 and called *The String of Pearls*, which told of a cannibal orgy that occurred daily at Mrs Lovett's pie shop at Bell-yard, close to the barber shop of Sweeney Todd, the demon barber of Fleet Street — 'one of the most celebrated shops for the sale of veal and pork pies that ever London produced. High and low, rich and poor, resorted to it, its fame had spread far and wide'. Like Wilkes's Fijians London lawyers parcelled up tidbits to take home to friends and relations. George Macfarren's mock-lyricism has a teasing tone: 'And well did they deserve their reputation, those delicious pies! there was about them a flavour never surpassed, and rarely equalled; the paste was of the most delicate construction, and impregnated with the aroma of a delicious gravy that defies description. Then the small portions of meat which they contained were so tender, and the fat and the lean so artistically mixed up, that to eat one of Lovett's pies was such a provocative to eat another, that many persons who came to lunch stayed to dine, wasting more than an hour, perhaps, of precious time....'[8]

There was the music hall song composed about 1830 by a man called Humphreys, 'The King of the Cannibal Islands'. Both its words and its tune were well known in a short time. At Nukuhiva in 1843 Herman Melville heard the band of the naval ship *United States* strike up the tune to welcome a state visit from Te Moana, the district chief. I have found the song referred to in five works of fiction or travel, the last of them in 1886. In this song the King has a nonsense name, there is a rollicking refrain of nonsense syllables ('Hokee pokee wonkee fum ...') and the story mocks him for ugliness, backward technology, vindictiveness, truculence, lack of affection or remorse, polygamy and infidelity. The King's name is Poonoo-wing-ke-wang Fli-bee-dee flo-bee-dee buskee-bang; he has a hundred wives, cooks fifty of them for a public feast. The other fifty run away to live with fifty lesser chiefs. The King has them killed but the wives return to haunt his dreams. That of course is not conscience but superstition. There were pantomime versions of this story in 1845 in London and in 1851 at Ashton-under-Lyme. In the last scene of both productions the King is turned into the stock role of Clown for the Harlequinade.[9]

To return to the seriously intended slanders:

In Harriet Martineau's poem which I will come back to the women live in kennels and an orphan girl would have died of neglect if a kind-hearted old man had not adopted her, in a gesture that belongs, one feels, to Dickens's England rather than Tahiti. There is some recognizable if ambivalent social protest in Miss Martineau's explanation: 'no one caring to nourish a helpless little creature of a sex not worthy to be offered in sacrifice, and of an age not ripe for cooking and beating fibre-cloth'.[10]

In such an onslaught of accusations against the island cultures, it is a relief to read in a novel published in 1838 an English sea-captain making a statement that allies him with another seaman, Herman Melville, when he describes Tahiti at dusk as 'a kind of vision of paradise, which has been witnessed by some with delight; and which others have since, under the garb of religion, and with promises of happiness hereafter, completely destroyed. They have broken down the barrier which innocence supported, and have inundated the island with vice, intemperance, and woe'.[11]

There were a dozen or so works, homiletic or didactic, or addressed to children, that celebrated several triumphs over the old religions, taken from Ellis: Pa'ati the priest of Mo'orea defying his gods, Pomare's conversion, his victory over the pagan army and his restraint in not punishing them, the destruction of the so-called 'idols', the chiefs' defiance of the gods on Hawaii even before the missionaries came, Kapiolani's entry into the crater of Kilauea to challenge Pele the goddess of the volcano.

There were moral tales of simplicity so child-like that only a child as simple-minded could not suspect the missionaries of duplicity: for example, a pagan priest on Huahine building a fence on a Sabbath is blinded by a twig and turns Christian.[12]

There are two dramatized conflicts between Christians and pagans, both unactable.* One of them is a dramatic poem, whose anonymous author says he does not approve of dramatic performances because of 'their evil and antichristian tendency'. The other is a play by a Scottish temperance activist John Dunlop.[12a] In both of them there is a secretly converted 'princess'; in both the opposition comes from a conspiracy of disloyal sub-chiefs; in both the princess's father is converted before the end of the play. In one, the Christians win because they are united and trust one another, while their enemies inevitably quarrel and intrigue among themselves. In Dunlop's play the Christians are led by Europeans who do not scruple to use a morally dubious opportunism. To assist the missionary, a Scottish seaman leads one army against another. It is his

* In fact the only dramatic treatment of the conflict which sees it in its tragic dimension, as a conflict within the souls of the islanders themselves, is Allen Curnow's *The Axe*, first performed in 1948 at Christchurch, but that lies outside the period I am covering.

shooting of a pagan priest that converts most of the chiefs to the Christian God and he offers them his knowledge of European weapons. But some missionaries were interested in the beliefs of their converts and there were sympathetic accounts: William Ellis wrote a verse epic 'Mahine,' of which only some lines have survived; his subject a Tahitian convert. Joseph Waterhouse, a missionary in Fiji in the eighteen-fifties, wrote an instructive book for young readers on Vah-ta-ah, a convert princess who changed husbands and returned for a while to her pagan belief before returning to the fold. Her story is told with sympathy and in an introduction Rev. Elijah Hoole writes of the 'new world opened up to us' by the discovery of the older religions.[13]

And Jesse Carey, in Fiji throughout the eighteen-sixties, wrote an epic of 117 cantos in Hiawatha rhythms of which the hero was Cakobau the convert warrior chief and the pre-Christian past is seen as a divine preparation for the coming of Christianity.[14]

The poem in heroic couplets titled *Tahiti, or The Voice of Truth* by A Lady (1845) is a plea for British intervention to protect Queen Pomare from French intimidation. Two other poems with the same purpose are notable for their Romantic tone. One of them was by Samuel Tamatoa Williams, son of the missionary martyr John Williams, and born in Ra'iatea where he spent his first eight years. It followed up a prose pamphlet by Williams on the French activities in Tahiti. The poem was published anonymously, titled *Pomare*: it acknowledges Byron as a technical model and dwells on Queen Pomare's youth, engaged in such innocent pursuits as decking her hair with flowers, watching the surf, swimming, paddling her canoe. Wandering alone she sees a young war chief leaning against a tree and falls in love with him. She is described as southern woman, not slow to melt like her northern sister: she flowers earlier in keeping with her climate.

> When love she feels, if woo'd, she soon is won.

Unlike her northern sister she is open and sincere and not coquettish.

The author's handling of one detail illustrates a change in treatment. Ellis describes her marriage, as a young woman known as Aimata; he notices a tear in her eye; it is, he says, because she is free to marry a man she loves, not someone chosen for her. To Mrs Mortimer, retelling the incident for children in *The Night of Toil* (1838) Aimata's tear was a Christian tear, a sign of the feeling that would not have been possible to her as a heathen. But for Samuel Tamatoa Williams, the tear is a warning of disaster:

> Not from distrust, or woman's ling'ring fear
> Of heart divided, springs that crystal tear;
> 'Tis deep emotion from some secret source,
> Which search defies when mind would trace its course,
> A dim foreshadowing of some after fate....[15]

Although it is a forewarning it is not an unmistakable Old Testament warning through dream or omen or writing on the wall, but a dim intimation from some unseen presence whose meaning will not be known till the event occurs. Its only effect is to produce a mild alarm, an appealing posture for a bride in the Romantic canon; but her accessibility to such intimations puts her on a level with English Romantic heroines, like Christabel or Madeline.

Sarah Ellis's poem shows more talent. She had satirical gifts as well as Romantic sympathies, and though she is writing with the same political purpose as Samuel Williams, the condition of England in the eighteen-forties is more in her mind than the innocence of a Tahitian bride; and the doctrines of Carlyle lie behind her claim that the missionary's occupation is higher even than that of the captain of industry. But he is an ally:

> Yet boast the wise a more enlightened plan
> To humanize the savage monster, man.
> It is to plant, wherever room is found,
> A thriving colony on foreign ground,
> And thus by European arts to win
> The wanderer of the woods to toil and spin.[16]

One notes that Mrs Ellis is as much concerned with colonization as with conversion; she acknowledges the injustice of land dealings in the past, and the evils that have followed European settlement. But she sees the missionary's task as one of spiritually equipping the islanders to cope with the evils that come with colonization. With some contradiction she sees the task as to teach the savage how to 'feel'; yet on the question of 'feeling', she casts her vote for the Romantic view of the savage — never in fact a flattering view — one who is passionate but ill-controlled, well-built and stupid. Here is Sarah Ellis:

Yet one thing brings this monster-life to view —
Whatever impulse stirs his soul is *true*.
True wrath, — true vengeance, — hatred, — passion — all
Which his fresh life-springs into action call.
All — how unlike sophisticated life! —
Is true to nature, and with feeling rife.

In fact Sarah Ellis confesses to a nostalgia for girlhood impressions of the Pacific taken from her reading:

Wild thoughts of freedom then my bosom fired.
A world of beauty filled with forms of light,
Pure as the morn, and hallowed as the night —
Mid the cool waters of the clear lagoon,
I saw them sporting in the waves at noon;
At eve I saw them in their blooming bowers,
Deck their dark hair with snow-white jasmine flowers,
Then mingle in the dance, unconscious still,
Of thought or purpose touched with human ill.[17]

It is a view of the islands that Southey had castigated and it owes something to William Mariner.

Mrs Ellis is less polemical than others when she admits to likeable qualities in Tahitians. James Wilson, of the *Duff*, and William Ellis had found them courteous and pleasant, but were swayed by their horror of the customs that shocked them. But to Mrs Favell Lee Mortimer, author of *The Night of Toil* (1838), the first book for children to celebrate missionary success, the contradiction was only apparent. Though they 'appeared merry and good-natured . . . they were thieves, liars, and murderers — could they be happy?'.[18] To Charles Wall, however, who set a children's Crusoe story on an island in the Solomons, there is a latent chivalry in South Sea islanders which emerges on contact with high-minded Europeans.[19] The Rev. N. W. Fiske, late Professor of Languages at Amherst College, though he found their religious practices repulsive, thought their myths 'sometimes invested with an air of lofty romance' that could be turned into legends rivalling those of 'Eastern nations'.[20]

William Mariner, the earliest of the beachcomber writers to be published, spent four years in Tonga from the year 1806 to 1810; his account of that time, published in 1817, was ghosted by Dr John Martin, and it was probably he who gave the book its consciously Romantic tone. If the island landscape in the late eighteenth century (in Bougainville for example) had been conceived in terms of post-Renaissance pastoral, it is presented by the early nineteenth-century writers as Romantic in one of two ways. One of them presents a dream-like landscape, rich in growth and colour against the calm of the waters within the reef. The other imposes a Celtic scenery of barren rocks, unscalable cliffs, sea-caves, and crashing waves. This is how John Martin sees the north-western coast of Vava'u:

'It happens that nature has assembled in this spot, not only the wildest profusion of the vegetable kingdom, over which the lofty *toa* tree stands pre-eminent, but also objects of another description, overhanging rocks, hollow-sounding caverns, and steep precipices, calculated to give an aspect as bold and sublime as the imagination can well conceive, and constituting a species of scenery, which, in proportion as it is more rare, is more admired by the natives.'[21] He describes the rock formations in terms of medieval architecture, and the characteristics of some of the chiefs in terms of Romantic preferences: Finau was 'passionately delighted with romantic scenery, poetry, and vocal concerts . . .', and of his uncle Finau Fisi Mariner says, 'His whole physiognomy was overshadowed by a cast of sublime melancholy . . .' — a Byronic figure.[22]

In Mariner there is a translated Tongan song, echoed in five of the works I have read. One can see why: it is a picture of an innocently sensuous life: the unmarried girls culling flowers from a burial-place and plaiting garlands for one another's hair, bathing and anointing one another with scented oil while the wind whistles in the branches of the *toa* and the surf roars below and there is the prospect of a night dance on the malae, and for the men, a battle next day: in the meantime they beg wreaths of flowers from scented girls on 'the flowery precipice of Mataloco'. There is a story that is repeated in English in several versions. In Mariner it concerns the daughter of a defeated rebel chief who has been killed: she is condemned to be killed but is saved by a young lover, a chief. He takes her to an unknown cave whose only entrance is under water and supplies her with food till they can escape to Fiji. 'How happy were they in this solitary retreat! . . . shut out from the world and all its cares and complexities.' Mariner's cave is in five works I have read, and even before Mariner had been published, Mary Russell Mitford imported a cave from the Hebridean coast (Fingal's Cave on Staffa). I don't think one needs Freud to see why the cave with its hidden entrance should have appealed. Byron has two caves, 'the grotto of the wave-worn shore' where the mutineer Torquil initiates the Polynesian Neuha into 'passion's devastating joy', and in the underwater cave she conceals him from the naval ship sent in pursuit.

Another myth that attracted Romantic attention was the *Bounty* mutiny. I am not interested in the copious *Bounty* literature for its own sake, since it concerns an act of rebellion by Europeans against Europeans and the establishment of a European colony free from an upper class, though not without a servant class. It is the race relations within the *Bounty* community that interests me. The mutineers looked on the six Polynesian men they took with them as servants, apparently sailing from Tahiti for the last time without giving them the opportunity to leave the ship. They divided Pitcairn into nine districts, one for each white man, none for the brown men; and though each mutineer had a wife, there were only three to be shared by the six Polynesians and one of those was claimed later by the mutineer whose wife died. The upshot was two rebellions of the landless Polynesians (one of them abortive) and a chain of murders pre-emptive and retaliatory. The result, ironically, was a community of God-fearing first- and second-generation Pitcairners, with a few Polynesian widows, presided over by the one surviving mutineer, the reformed patriarch Alexander Smith, who reverted to his born name John Adams. To Captain Mayhew Folger, who found them, and to England and America it seemed to be the innocent plain-living community that the early visitors thought they had found in Polynesia and the variation on it that the missionaries were trying to establish, a sabbath-observing Bible-reading community. The finding of Pitcairn seemed to illustrate several morals: the fruit of man's disobedience, the mysterious ways of Providence and the operations of grace.[23] As John Barrow, Secretary of the Navy and later historian of the mutiny, put it in 1815: 'O happy people! happy in your sequestered state! . . . May no civilized barbarian lay waste your peaceful abodes; no hoary proficient in swinish sensuality rob you of that innocence and simplicity which it is peculiarly your present lot to enjoy!' Perhaps I should add that the civilized barbarian he had in mind was Captain David Porter of the United States Navy who laid waste the habitations of the Taipi in Nukuhiva in 1813.[24]

Mary Russell Mitford was the first to tackle the story of the *Bounty* mutiny: and her motive was in part to remove a blot from the name of the 'highly respectable family' of Fletcher Christian. Several years before Byron, she makes him a Byronic hero who is haunted by his crime and goes mad, laughing in fits and seeing visions of Bligh when his first child dies at birth. As well he might . . . because in Miss Mitford's version, it was for the sake of the baby that he engineered the mutiny. It wasn't that he wanted to mutiny but he had got Iddeah pregnant, and unless he takes her with him, those 'Arreoys' will kill the baby. Bligh won't let her come with the ship. What else could Christian do? He dies plunging over the cliff into the tide to spare his second child the effects of the curse that is on him. Miss Mitford makes the surviving patriarch the hero, under the Celtic name Fitzallan. In her account (got indirectly from Adams's story to Mayhew Folger, published in the *Naval Chronicle*, 1809, which is now known to be misleading) all the Tahitian men were killed by the Tahitian women in revenge for the murders of their English husbands, and that was the result of the rebellion of the Tahitian men led by a weak-minded youth called Tupia and morally quite distinct from the noble, if fatal, mutiny led by Christian. A double standard.[25]

Byron too removes Christian from the central role and gives that to a Celt — Torquil from the Hebrides. Christian in this version dies fighting the men from the vessel come to arrest him, the *Pandora*, even firing the top button of his tunic when his ammunition runs out, before he leaps to his death. Torquil and his bride remain in the cave.

Byron sees pre-missionary Tahiti as a happy place free from Europe's ills. He cheerfully accepts that the islanders are sinners but the sins of Europe are compounded.

> True, they had vices — such are Nature's growth —
> But only the Barbarian's — we have both:
> The sordor of civilization, mixed
> With all the savage which man's fall hath fixed.[26]

There is an anonymous and improving book for children published in 1829 in Amherst, Massachusetts, *The Story of Aleck*, that draws the appropriately pious conclusions; and a novel of 1819 by Charles Sargent, *The Life of Alexander Smith*, that fills in gaps in the accounts then known in a way that idealizes the mutineers, and I suspect does so to preserve a magnanimous self-image, since the reader is drawn to identify with them. The mutineers are exonerated from suspicion of taking the Polynesian men against their will, since they picked them up adrift at sea, and when they became homesick on Pitcairn, the mutineers built them a boat and gave them sailing directions to Tahiti. Thus a paternalistic relation is presented between the mutineers and the Polynesians.[27]

More interesting is Frederick Chamier. He writes with a seaman's understanding of the reasons the mutineers chose to remain in the Pacific, and he makes the Tahitians, as it were, natural Christians before the missionaries ruined them. When Adams is flogged for desertion his wife clings round his neck, offering her own back instead. Adams's taio, his name-exchange friend, leads a chant of protest against the flogging. But a naval officer cannot condone mutiny; and neither does Chamier approve of the deception of the Tahitian men when the *Bounty* sailed from Tahiti. So his mutineers are corrupted by their crime and the Tahitians in turn become restless. Christian plans to enslave them, fearing mutiny. But mutiny begets quarrel and so the Tahitians quarrel among themselves. 'From virtuous savages they had become half-civilised monsters'. And so to the end of the cycle. Yet it is clear that Chamier shows some sympathy with the Englishmen's fear of the Tahitians becoming their masters.[28]

There was another way to civilize the Polynesians than by Christianity. It is proposed in Harriet Martineau's *Dawn Island*, a story published in Manchester in 1845. That way is Free Trade and it is proposed by a trading captain who wants to wean them from human sacrifice. ' "Lay before them," said the captain seriously, "an axe, and a knife, and a looking-glass, and a garment of cotton." ' The captain sails away, pleased at introducing 'the principles and incitements of civilization among a puerile people. . . .' 'It warmed my heart and filled my head to see how these children of nature were clearly destined to be carried on some way toward becoming men and Christians by my bringing Commerce to their shores.'

One recalls that when William Ellis wrote of the benefits of Tahitians adopting European clothing, he said that it not only provided an incentive to work, it had opened a market for British manufacturers.[29]

I want to look at some American works that have struck me as notable. The earliest is a novel published in 1828, written by a clergyman who had never been west of the Rocky Mountains, Timothy Flint's *Arthur Clenning*. In that novel there is a woman character, vaguely Polynesian in description, native of an island north of Australia. The hero and his loved one, who have been shipwrecked, save this woman from some people with woolly heads and high cheekbones who are likened to representations of Satan and are seen dancing round a fire. The American couple call her Rescue and immediately take her into the captivity of domestic service since she is 'theirs by indissoluble ties'. This novel is not only a democratic success story in which a manly young American wins an English earl's daughter, and her estate, it contains a myth of slavery. Twenty-five years before *Uncle Tom's Cabin*, Rescue has the qualities of the slave domestic of that novel. She fondles her mistress's locks and says 'Oh! God make you handsome'; she points to her master, 'He good; but poor Rescue bad, silly, black.' When she is pleased she capers and snaps her fingers, exclaiming 'Eh! Eh!'. She provides them with endless amusement in her efforts to imitate their ways. Back in Illinois she refuses to listen to emancipationists who tell her she is free. When a young American Indian chief proposes to her, the hero of the novel allows the match only on condition he leaves his people and comes to work on one of his farms.[30]

There is a myth of colonialism in Fenimore Cooper's novel *The Crater*, published in England as *Mark's Reef*, a late work of Cooper's about a model colony founded on an uninhabited Pacific island and usually discussed as a commentary on American society. The aspect that interests me is the relationship with the savage inhabitants of a neighbouring island. The bad chief Waally who raids the colony is a usurper and Mark, the governor of the colony, employs force to restore the legitimate chief and, being too lenient the first time, has to attack Waally again. The profitable sandalwood trade is restored: and a term of the peace agreement is that the colony gets a hundred native lads as seamen apprentices, to be held as hostages against the good behaviour of their parents, as well as a hundred able-bodied men as labourers to be paid in beads and trifles.[31]

There is another tradition in South Sea stories, that of Baron Munchausen. The author of the short spoof of travellers' tales, called *Gulliver Revived* and published in 1785, was a German émigré Rudulf Erich Raspe who had assisted Georg Forster in translating his *Voyage Round the World* into German. In the following year the book was greatly enlarged with further adventures written by the publishers' hacks. By 1830 the *Surprising Adventures of Baron Munchausen*, under this or other titles, had gone into more than thirty editions in Britain and the United States. It is doubtful if any literate seaman had not read it or heard of it.

This is relevant to a book published in New York in 1832, which contains the narrative of a voyage prospecting for trade in the western Pacific in 1830 made by a New York captain Benjamin Morrell who was known after his death, amongst those who talked of these things, as the biggest liar in the Pacific.[32]

His book is an account of four voyages in the Atlantic, the Antarctic, and the Pacific over a period of ten years. It was not written until the end of the fourth voyage and he admits to bolstering his memories by reference to the library of earlier navigators, like Cook and Vancouver, one of his backers had lent him. There are two other accounts of the Pacific voyage, one that cannot be seen as independent, that of his wife Abby Jane, whom he smuggled aboard in a bread-locker against the wishes of the owners, and a log written by his teenage brother-in-law, John Keeler. Keeler's log enables us to detect particular variations that Morrell made and to speculate why.

The key-piece of Morrell's narrative is a 'massacre' that occurred on Kilinailau, a ring of coral islets, east-north-east of Buka. Morrell claims to have established good relations with the people. He cleared bush to build a station for curing beche de mer, the tropical sea slug eaten by Chinese gourmets; but was the victim of a surprise attack in which several of his men were killed or wounded and some left behind. Morrell sailed to Manila to rearm the ship and take on extra crew for a punitive expedition; he returned to Kilinailau, destroyed the islanders' fleet, bombarded a village, and claims to have bought an island for his curing-station. The one survivor of the crew who had been left behind, Leonard Shaw, joined the ship. But they were continually harassed by the local people and packed up after a month with their cargo uncompleted.

On the way out Morrell captured three men. The first, from Kilinailau, died on board. The next was picked up off one of the Witu islands north of New Britain; they called him Sunday. The third was picked up off an atoll whose location Morrell kept secret because of its commercial prospects, but has been identified as the Ninigo group north of New Guinea.[33] They called this man Monday. Both Sunday and Monday, a Melanesian and a Micronesian who could not speak one another's languages, were displayed for a charge at Tammany Hall, New York, dressed in 'clothes similar to those of the coloured men of this country'.[34] It was to accompany this exhibition that Keeler published an altered version of his log, probably ghosted, as I think was the accompanying account of the sufferings of Leonard Shaw, the seaman left behind in captivity on Kilinailau.

The existence of three versions of the same events throws some light on Morrell's purposes. I will confine myself to three notable cases of departure from John Keeler's manuscript, which I assume to be as close to the truth as Keeler saw it at the time.

In May 1830 the 'Antarctic' passed Nukuoro, the southernmost of the Carolines. Keeler says: 'Saw not the least signs of any inhabitants but we expect There must be i[n]habitants as there is not an island in the Pacific ocean that has any cocoanuts on but what you will find Negros on.'[35] On 6 September the ship passed this island again. They were met by canoes, from one of which a man made a speech, broke a stick in two, put one part in the bow of the canoe and the other in the sea. The canoes made towards the shore, were joined by other canoes, where weapons were distributed, and the reinforced fleet sailed towards the ship. The 'Antarctic' read hostile intentions and fired, killing and wounding about twenty. It is notable how these events have changed in Morrell's version. The true account of the May visit is omitted and the events of September are shifted to replace it. But what is omitted from that encounter is the part that is most interesting — the ceremonial gesture of the chief breaking the stick, a gesture that indicates that something was meant to be communicated about territorial rights and the possibility of the visitors landing. In Morrell's account of the May visit, the people of Nukuoro at first engaged in friendly trading with the Americans and later attacked without warning. But rather than slaughter 'these ignorant misguided people' the Americans sailed away.

One now sees the reason for the changes. These events have been rewritten to serve as a dramatic prelude to the events of September, which are in fact the same events repeated with the variation that the ship is said to be becalmed and at the mercy of the attackers. 'I now repented of my forbearance on a former occasion . . . I regretted it for their own sake; for at that time a slight chastisement would have been sufficient. . . . ' So the rearrangement of events serves the double purpose of showing that savage friendliness is not to be trusted and that Morrell's humaneness was not only misplaced but obliged him to be more severe in the end. It is the syndrome one might call 'Pity Wasted; or, A Shot in Time Saves Nine.' [36]

There are two other occasions where Morrell's account of events notably differs from Keeler's log. One of them concerns the events on Kilinailau. Keeler's log is less detailed. On their third day at the group, the Americans went ashore — on low islands of coral sand and rock whose soil and vegetation are vulnerable to strong winds and high seas — and began to clear away bush to build a house. Morrell tells an incredible story of his cultivating the ground, the natives' anxiety at his disturbance of the soil, and his assurance that he was planting a garden 'from generous and disinterested motives' with the seeds of a dozen or two varieties of temperate-climate fruit and vegetables (potatoes, pumpkins, cabbages, apples, and the like). When the people understand that this effort has been undertaken entirely for their benefit, 'the whole welkin rang with their joyous shouts'.

Morrell claims that such spontaneous acknowledgement of his magnanimity was repeated nearly two days later by the chiefs. When the armorers' tools were stolen on the day after the reported sowing of seeds, Morrell took an armed party ashore to demand their return, but found his party surrounded by three or four hundred islanders. Nevertheless he takes dramatic command of the situation, forcing them to disarm by threatening the life of the high chief at the point of pistols and cutlasses. He then takes the chiefs aboard as hostages. The taking of hostages, at least, is confirmed by Keeler who tells us that the head chief jumped overboard and swam ashore. This was during the night before the apparently retaliatory attack that Morrell called the massacre. In Morrell's version, which perhaps draws on Hawkesworth's account of Cook's arrest of the Tahitian chiefs, he provides his prisoners with everything they might need and they are so pleased with his handsome treatment of them that in the morning they thank him profusely. The incident heightens the treachery of the events that follow.[37]

Another example appears to be a gratuitous tribute to Morrell's own geniality. He engages in a rhapsody on the admirable qualities of the people of Truk (which he named Bergh's Island after the New York shipbuilder who was one of his backers) — they were more thorough and diligent than other Pacific islanders, keener to work, and even had a law against lying in bed after sunrise. It was an opinion that found its way into the first two editions of Findlay's Directory for Navigation (1851 and 1870), and it conflicted directly with the opinion of Andrew Cheyne, an industrious and censorious Scot who came to Truk for sandalwood fourteen or fifteen years later and described the people as 'too lazy to work' besides being cruel and treacherous.[38] All that is common to the two opinions is the criterion by which the Trukese were judged — their willingness to provide labour for western commercial enterprises. By a sort of Gresham's Law by which bad opinions deserve more attention than good, Findlay preferred Cheyne's opinion and warned captains to be wary. (Findlay, by the way, was one of the reference works on which one of the later writers of boys' adventure fiction relied for his knowledge of which islands were dangerous to visitors.)

But Cheyne's opinion can at least be trusted to be based on experience. Keeler's log shows that for the dates given by Morrell for his visit to Truk, the 'Antarctic' was several hundred miles further west, at Tamatam, now called Pulap, where they did not land but engaged in friendly shipside trading no more notable than at other islands. There is even doubt whether Morrell set foot on Truk at all.[39] When Morrell goes on to propose a commercial venture to Truk that would return a profit of five hundred per cent, one sees the rhapsody as an exercise in writing a company prospectus; except that the venture is one that Morrell himself cannot have seriously entertained. So the whole passage seems to have no other purpose than to inspire confidence in his ability to establish cooperative relations with islanders in order to offset doubts raised by the hostilities at Kilinailau.[40]

Morrell's style is florid and is probably his own, though one of his disgruntled backers, Captain William Skiddy, says loosely that his account was 'written and published' by Samuel Woodworth, a New York literary all-rounder. But this may mean no more than that Woodworth wrote a play based on the 'massacre' which had twenty performances at the Bowery Theatre.[41] Woodworth's son sailed with Morrell on his next voyage as captain's clerk.[42]

Clearly Morrell uses the devices of fiction. It is less obvious that the style used for his account of the 'massacre' belongs to a genre that carries its built-in preconceptions. Morrell's crew speak in the heroic rhetoric of popular adventure fiction: the prose is full of its cliches: 'sell your lives dearly!' — there are blood-curdling war-whoops, bloody fangs, hell-hounds, well-directed fire mowing down their ranks, sable demons biting the dust (six black men for every white), arrows protruding from a corpse like the quills of a porcupine. But this is 1832, before Captain Marryat and the British boys' novels, thirty years before the American dime novels; it is a style too facile for Fenimore Cooper. The answer lies in a genre that has been called the Indian captivity narrative. It has been described by Roy Harvey Pearce.[43]

It was a form of narrative that first appeared in New England in the late seventeenth century; a puritan account of the sufferings of a white person taken into Indian captivity. The whole series of events was seen as a trial sent by the Lord and the Indians throughout are seen as devils or as agents of the Devil. The narrator shows no sense of common humanity. The early captivity narratives were based on actual experience, but the form developed its own conventions and, by the late eighteenth century, captivities had become a kind of imagined adventure story. The convention of the inhuman Indians remained. It is this assumption that Morrell can count on in his readers' expectations. The story of Leonard Shaw, included in his book, is in fact an exact replica of the form.

Morrell's book made some impact. It was followed up by his wife's account. There was Woodworth's play; there was a children's book published in Boston. Edgar Allan Poe sent up Morrell's posture of having the complete confidence of the island peoples while arming himself to the teeth. That is in the *Narrative of Arthur Gordon Pym*, in which Poe takes four paragraphs verbatim from Morrell. Years later Melville bought the accounts of this voyage and Morrell's next, though not till after he had written *Typee* and *Omoo*.[44]

The account of Morrell's last Pacific voyage in 1835 provides a compendium of western exploitative attitudes in the unmissioned region of Melanesia.[45] Few have noticed that this book contains what must be the earliest of the several hoax accounts of journeys to the interior of New Guinea. There is a good deal of hoax, not all of it disguised, but there is sufficient truth to demand serious attention. There is no doubt that the clipper brig 'Margaret Oakley' called at Sydney in April 1835, and I have been assured by an ANU linguist that the word-lists collected at various places are good Austronesian words, even though my informant was not prepared to comment on the exact local provenance of the words. If the facts cannot be confidently separated from the hoax, that isn't important. What is important is that the attitudes shown were acceptable to the self-esteem of the writer, of his publisher — who had also published Morrell — and to the American reading public in 1844. The account was written four or five years after Morrell's death by a man who had sailed with him, joining his ship as a college graduate no more than twenty, attracted it seems by Morrell's reputation, as many gifted and adventurous young men were. His name was Thomas Jefferson Jacobs. Clearly he admired Morrell's skill as a tall-story teller.

It was over two years before Morrell could find backers with confidence to equip him for another voyage, and these ones sent two company representatives with him in a small brig so leaky that it was extensively repaired at Mauritius. Perhaps it was memories of Kilinailau or some insane intention that caused the captain to use the opportunity to have the ship so well armed that local people suspected he was entering the slave trade or piracy. The only use he made of arms however was to intimidate or dominate.

Morrell was helped in his venture by his good relations with the Melanesian he had captured in the Witu Islands, Sunday. The Micronesian Monday who resented his capture had died. Sunday appears to have cheerfully accommodated himself and was now revealed as 'Prince Telum-by-by-Darco', the ruler of Narage, one of the islands in the Witu group. Home again on Narage, he treated his American friends as privileged guests and himself told tall stories about New York. He also undertook to collect a cargo of shell and sea-slug for them. It was presumably this assistance that freed the fast well-armed little vessel to engage on a circuit of irresponsible knight-errantry around the coasts of New Britain, New Ireland, and Manus.

The gamut of attitudes of the Americans to their native hosts can be generally described as genial imposture, which can be illustrated from a number of incidents, of which I select one or two that are possible — not necessarily true, or even always credible. A standard tactic in meeting the menace of hostile inhabitants brandishing weapons at the water's edge was for the crew to intimidate them with an insane rumpus beginning with three cheers, followed by a cacophony from the ship's band of drums, horns, and the boatswain's whistle. This might cause the natives to retreat into the forest; perhaps to return with a present. The procedure would end in the ritual chewing of betel-nut by the captain and the chief. The visitors claimed to have come from the moon or the sun, and might engage in quack doctoring of the sick or wounded. The captain sometimes intervened in local disputes, threatening to use his gun. At Ndende in the Santa Cruz group he fends off an attack by trickery with mirrors, blinding the attackers with refracted light, and igniting blue-light and fire-crackers. Once they fire wildly over a trivial cause and observe the grief of a father whose two sons were shot; they had come to buy trinkets for their sweethearts. The crew shed facile tears as the distracted father, having lifted his sons' corpses into his canoe, drifts in the dusk through a break in the reef to the open sea. They are on good terms with the son of a chief on New Britain and are guests at his wedding, and they visit Darco again. Yet the favours they receive don't rule out coveting the land. Passing Erromanga Jacobs thinks of conquering the people with a small force and bringing them to 'the most complete subjection'. A proprietorial attitude comes out as they approach Western New Guinea. The people they call 'Malay' are condemned as cruel exploiters of the blacks, and the Dutch are blamed for laying claim to Western Papua. 'We all have a right to this country in common and a vast field lies open for the settlement and trade of civilized people.' Generally the impression is left of a benign but cavalier attitude to people ripe for expropriation and easily dominated if one knows how to handle them.

Probably Morrell and Jacobs, as well as Mariner and Melville, have gone into the several popular novels that appeared in the eighteen-forties like *Old Slade* or *Torrey's Narrative*.[46] They are male fantasies of domination, all of them drawing to some extent on the experience of the American whaling industry, all of them to some degree spurious in their claims to be authentic, all prurient and boastful. Old Slade, for example, buys an island and rules it by a mixture of intimidation and manipulating the islanders' superstitions, arranging an eclipse for them. He plans to marry the chief's ten-year-old daughter when she turns twelve.

Some incidents appear to be part of an emerging formula. The recurrent features are these: A ship is threatened or attacked by fierce savages, openly or by trickery, usually in the islands as yet unaffected by Christian missions — the Marquesas, the Tuamotus, the Kingsmills (Kiripati), and Wallis Island. Great play is made of cannibalism. Sailors at first act humanely or give advantage to their enemies in battle rather than shed their blood; but they come to regret it and in the end have to defend themselves ruthlessly. The seamen sometimes play on superstition or credulity. The hero has a mistress seldom of lesser rank than chief's daughter, through whom he may inherit land and status. There is often a routine observation contrasting the carefree contentment of the sailor's current situation and the harsh life of wage slavery in his own country. One can sometimes recognize the source of some experiences — Mariner, for example, for the incident in *Harry Martingale* where the Marquesans seize the vessel and burn it, having killed all the crew except the hero who is favourably treated; or Hawkesworth's version of Wallis's log where the sailors' attention is distracted before the attack by the lascivious gestures of girls in canoes. One can see Melville as the model for *Torrey's Narrative* in which he, like Melville, lives with a Marquesan tribe, takes part in a war, but goes better than Melville in sharing in a cannibal feast — and confesses to liking the food.

And because this is the logical thematic place for it, there was a fantasy serialized in an English working-class newspaper in 1869. It purports to be American, but I cannot find evidence of its having been published as a separate book in the United States, even among the many hundreds of dime novels published by the firm Beadle and Adams. It plagiarizes

Melville, but the author does not know the Pacific and his indulgence in fantasy is unashamed. I think some of his other sources can be recognized from the literature I have already cited. The teller claims to have jumped ship at 'Oitahu' (Vaitahu on Tahuata). He marries a fourteen-year-old princess who rules the northern part of the island. The king is in fact an escaped Australian convict, tattooed, who kicks his wives out of his way; and they treat him with greater respect the more harshly he treats them. Jack the hero is tattooed and in a war in which there are many gruesome atrocities and the Typees and the Hiva Oans are put to flight, Jack rescues an enemy princess. He escapes with her by hiding in an ocean cave with an undersea entrance. He marries her, he beats further opponents and marries a third girl, an English captain's daughter; though he lets her know that Marquesan women are superior. The convict king dies, and Jack leads the people to victory over the Typees, subjugates all the islands of the group and rules for twenty years. He goes back to the United States for a holiday but looks forward to returning to his wives and children.[47]

Perhaps I should add that the newspaper in which this serial appeared struck me as an ancestor of the *News of the World*: its circulation was advertised as 150,000.[48]

The attitudes of Thomas Jefferson Jacobs contribute to a boys' adventure story published in Boston in 1851, written by James Bowman, later a San Francisco newspaper editor. The book, which went into three American editions and five English, was titled *The Island Home*, published under two pseudonyms. An incident in Jacobs is in fact sceptically referred to where Morrell ratifies a treaty of peace by chewing betel with a king standing more than seven feet, and his hundred warriors of like height, on an island apparently off the south coast of New Britain. Bowman's novel is a story of the adventures of seven youths, six of them white and one Polynesian, after being marooned by mutineers on an uninhabited island. In the first part of novel they learn how to survive, Crusoe style, with the help of the skills of Euilo the Polynesian, who is a prince and no Friday since he is treated as equal to the American boys. Their adventures on the island are educational. Bowman has read widely and imparts his learning of the biology and geography of the South Pacific — it is what had been done in other tropical regions by J. D. Wyss in *Swiss Family Robinson* (1812) and Frederick Marryat in *Masterman Ready* (1841). There are other recognizable sources — Wilkes on Fiji, and a book only just published, E. M. Lucett's *Rovings in the Pacific*, an account of twelve years as a merchant trader in the eastern Pacific. Lucett tells of a visit to Fangatau or Angatau in the eastern Tuamotus — which by a typographical error appears as Angatan — to a people said by the people on the nearest island to be fierce and cannibal, and instead finds them shy and friendly, even jolly. He called them 'a harmless inoffensive race' and ' "Nature's unsophisticated children" '. But the reputation for ferocity was irresistible, and Bowman uses Angatan as the cannibal island to which an American trading ship is driven off course. They have a Tahitian Christian chief as a passenger. On shore they find a hideous priest who wants the visitors sacrificed. Arthur who speaks Tahitian preaches to the crowd; and he discovers that the local chief's wife is dreaming of a humane religion like the one he preaches. It is by moving her feelings that Arthur persuades the chief to spare his aunt who is about to be put to death because she is old. The chief helps them escape from the priest, and the Tahitian chief risks his life in helping them get away from the inhuman looking men dancing around a bonfire in front of their hideous idols. So the pro-missionary elements of this situation are these: the loyal Christian native saves the whites from the untamed savages, who are not only needing, but at least one of them awaiting, the rescue of Christianity.[49]

The main plot of the book reinforces the myth of tutelage. The seven youths become involved in the political affairs of Eiulo and his family. Eiulo's grandfather, who is the legitimate ruler of an island, is under attack from a dissident younger brother, incited by some pot-stirring French beachcombers. After a series of captures and escapes and interventions, the rebel is killed by a faithful chief Wakatta, and the youths are rewarded for their support. What follows is a myth of easy assumption of privilege. Wakatta offers Max a breadfruit plantation, and a granddaughter as wife if he will settle. Eiulo noticing how much the visitors like rock oysters places a rahui on them, so that they alone can eat them. The Europeans by virtue of siding with legitimacy have been given immediate equality with the local upper class, but their attitudes are patronizing: 'Max has taken a great fancy to Wakatta, whom he emphatically pronounces "a trump," "a regular brick," besides bestowing upon him a variety of other elegant and original designations, of the like complimentary character.' . . . 'Browne's prejudices against the "heathen savages" have been greatly softened by what he has seen of these natives, and he says that "if the rest of them are equally well-behaved, one might manage to get along with them quite comfortably." '[50]

This is benign, and implies a possibility of friendly partnership. The attitude of R. M. Ballantyne, who used *The Island Home* as the model for his first adventure story *The Coral Island*, is more severe. Ballantyne's biographer Eric Quayle tells us that his main source of knowledge of the Pacific was a popularization of Wilkes and several other books published in London by Thomas Nelson, his own publisher.[51] He tells us too that later Ballantyne planned to produce a series of adventure stories by which working class youths could be instructed in religious truths as well as popular history, geography, and science. The first of these was *Gascoyne the Sandalwood Trader* in 1863, but the series did not sell, and when it was revived in 1869 it was aimed at boys of the middle class, who were more responsive. New issues in this series continued until the beginning of World War One.[52] Ballantyne's main rival in the field was W. H. G. Kingston, a man who was an exponent of colonization, of missions, and of missions for seamen, a member of a vigilante Rifle Corps ready to engage with Chartists in the late eighteen-forties and a volunteer home defence corps when British troops were engaged on such frontiers as Crimea and India. He made some memorable statements: this from a public lecture delivered in 1849:

'As far as it is permitted to man to comprehend the decrees of the Almighty, we have reason to believe that to the Anglo-Saxon race has been awarded the office of peopling the yet uninhabited portions of the globe, of spreading the arts of civilization, and more than all, of promulgating the true faith of Christ among the lands of the heathen.'[53]

And this from an article extolling missions that appeared in a journal that he edited: 'What more noble occupation than to bear the tidings of Salvation to a perishing people?'[54]

In 1880, expecting to die shortly, he wrote a farewell letter to the editor and readers of the *Boy's Own Paper*, in the tone of a retirement speech, looking back on a life well spent.[55] For what it is worth, a questionnaire put to boys between the ages of eleven and nineteen by the Royal Empire Society in 1884 came up with Kingston as favourite author for the second greatest proportion of the boys asked. (Dickens was first.)[56] Ballantyne was favourite for only a sixth of those who answered. Nevertheless of Kingston's 160 odd books, twenty of them set in the Pacific, only six went into new editions in the twentieth century, and none later than 1934. Ballantyne wrote six novels or collections of tales set in the Pacific, and of them *The Coral Island*, amazingly, had gone into fifty-odd English editions by 1975, not counting reprints and abridgements, as well as several translations. It is a book no better and no worse in its preposterous white supremacy than many others of its time, set on the various frontiers of British expansion (historical and geographical), whether Africa, North America, India, the Spanish Main, the Java Sea, or the Pacific, and it is matter of wonder that it should continue to be read and rated as a children's classic. I imagine it is because of its long educational first section, which is about three boys learning how to survive on their own on an uninhabited island, and contains interesting information about sharks, crabs, coral, the banyan tree, the coconut, water spouts, a tidal wave, a storm at sea.

It is in the second half of the book that attitudes to Pacific island cultures are revealed. Two parties of savages come to the island, one in pursuit of the other. The boys are immediately on their guard. The eldest boy Jack says: 'This I know that all the natives of the South Sea Islands are fierce cannibals, and they have little respect for strangers'.[57] The leader of the pursuers can be morally judged by his features which are a combination of Marquesan, Fijian, and Melanesian models that the English middle class could only see as repulsive or comic: he is massive, mop-haired, coal-black, tattooed from head to foot and his face smeared with red and white paint; and he is described as 'the most terrible monster I ever beheld'.

Gallantry towards women and the protection of the weak are part of the self-image of these boys and when the victorious chief threatens a young woman of striking modesty and gentleness of demeanour, the boys leap into the fray and reverse the situation so that the captives are released and their captors taken prisoner. But the new victors, no less heathen, need educating in civilized behaviour. One of them goes to cut a slice from the dead chief's thigh and Jack orders him to desist. When he refuses Jack appeals to the good chief who raises his club to 'dash out the brains' of the man, but Jack again intervenes. In the excitement it is easy to overlook how quickly Jack the uninvited ally and benefactor has taken command, first by indirect rule and then direct. It is a question of sovereignty. When the visitors leave the island the only one to show regret at parting is the modest and gentle Avatea, but 'the fine manly moral tone' that an Edinburgh clergyman found in Ballantyne is upheld by a sentence that precludes any possibility of serious or equal friendship between Avatea and the boys: 'Going up to Jack, she put out her flat little nose to be rubbed, and thereafter paid the same compliment to Peterkin and me.' She thus becomes desexed — a charmingly childish

figure to be patronized.[58] She is repeatedly ridiculed by Peterkin.
We have had three of the four sets of participants we observed in George Forster; the good and the bad islanders, and the good whites (who are the boys). Now the bad whites come on the scene, the sandalwooders turned pirate, who capture one of the boys, Ralph, and take him off to another island inhabited by unredeemed savages. One of the sandalwooders, Bloody Bill, is a more sympathetic character than the others, and his experience is used to confirm Ralph's intuitive moral reactions to the islanders. In fact what is notable in this myth of domestication is the identity of attitudes of the good and the bad whites. The pirates meet a native missionary schooner at sea, but they do not harm it because they know that 'the only place among the southern islands where a ship can put in and get what she wants in comfort is where the gospel has been sent to'. One of the worst of them makes the point which is made by the novel itself: 'The South-Sea islanders are such incarnate fiends that they are the better for being tamed, and the missionaries are the only men who can do it.' [59]

Nevertheless, the native missionaries are presented as figures of ridicule; most of them are naked, and those that are dressed wear incongruous clothing like a black beaver hat or a straw hat with a swallow-tail coat over bare legs. They speak an Uncle Tom English that could be expected to amuse young readers.

Ralph tacitly accepts the truth of the pirate's statement in a morally ambiguous episode that follows. The ship needs fresh water and sends a boat ashore to a small island. It is met by 'a band of naked blacks' brandishing weapons. The captain fires 'a withering shower of grape', and there is a horrifying description of the mutilated and the dead who have turned the stream red with blood. Nevertheless, the watering party goes upstream and fills its casks. Ralph ponders that the pirates as well as the savages need taming; but he has accepted the terrorism as the price of the water.

Bill delivers to Ralph a long sermon in which he claims to have witnessed all the horrors of which the pagan islanders are guilty. Mothers throw their babies to an eel which they worship; the 'areoi' are ready for any wickedness man can devise; the people are without natural feeling. It is what the missionary writers were saying twenty years earlier but this is addressed to boys, and it appears at a time when a newer kind of missionary were interesting themselves in the old mythologies and championing islanders against the exploitation of traders and labour traders.

Ralph returns to the island and the three boys set out on another rescue mission, this time for the sake of Avatea, whose father Tararo, the good chief they had helped earlier, is preparing to sacrifice her because she wants to marry against his wishes. It is a Christian chief she wants to marry.

The boys sail to Tararo's island Mango, where the missionaries already have a footing, and they are met by a 'mild-looking native' wearing a straw hat and a respectable European suit, making a low bow, a Christian. But Ballantyne's readers are educated in the appropriate attitude to the domesticated native when one of the boys, a swaggering little white-supremacist, says, 'We may as well come it as strong over these black chaps as we can', and speaking contemptuously to half a dozen inhabitants on the deck, gives them a tray of broken biscuits and a can of water. 'Then, thrusting his hands into his pockets, he walked up and down the deck with an enormous swagger, whistling vociferously.'[60]

On the heathen side of Mango the boys witness Tararo engaged in preparation for a cannibal feast in a temple strewn with bones and skulls. There is a huge pile of fruit and vegetables (as in a Tongan ceremony of harvest distribution, described by Cook). Avatea is placed on top of it, waiting to be sacrificed. With the help of the native missionary from the other side of the island the boys rescue her, and after recaptures and further escapes Avatea is free to marry her Christian lover, a chief from another island. This outcome has been made possible because Tararo himself has been converted to Christianity: there is a nice racist point in the detail that it is not a native missionary but a white missionary from a passing ship who has converted him. Even when the boys are in process of saving Avatea, Peterkin sees her as a comic figure, 'just like a black owl blinking in the sunshine'; and when she snores, he says 'Perchance she dreameth of her black Apollo!'[61]

So that these two books, *The Island Home* and *The Coral Island*, are myths of white supremacy in the forms of easy assumption of privilege or of domestication. There were others like them. Double standards operate; even in the language. When a chief dodges a blow from Jack's staff he is said to be as 'agile as a cat'; when Jack does the same, he is able to 'easily evade' the chief's heavy weapon.[62] In Ballantyne's later novel *Gascoyne the Sandalwood Trader* Henry Stuart knocks down Keona, a youth who is wounded in one arm, presses on his throat till he is blue in the face, and holds the point of a knife to his chest. This is treated as just but when Keona gives one of the crew a backhander on the nose this is said to be cowardly. In this same novel there is a stupid Christian girl Kekupoopi who is never addressed except by some comic version of her name — Kickup, Puppy, or Poopy; whom a little white boy describes as 'a lower species of human natur'.' When she sits beside this boy in church he looks at her with 'a mingled expression of disgust and contempt' and edges away. But he reproves her when she laughs in church. Kekupoopi doesn't mind: she had been brought up very cruelly by a stepmother who had pulled her hair out in handfuls and 'beat her nose flat (which was adding insult to injury for it was flat by nature)'. This girl is presented in terms of the comic southern negro, using the locutions of Mrs Harriet Beecher Stowe's Topsy. In this novel the Christians have an army led by a Norwegian, to defend themselves against the unconverted, and he has a servant he calls Sambo. 'Sambo was not his proper name, but his master, regarding him as being the embodiment of all the excellent qualities that could by any possibility exist in the person of a South Sea islander, had bestowed upon him the generic name of the dark race.' [63]

'Sunk at Sea' a tale published in 1874, ends with a reassuringly ridiculous picture of the Fijian ruler 'Thackombau' at church in an odd assortment of European clothing, a lady's shawl around his loins and a nightcap on his head. (Cakobau, a man of substance as a political leader in a time of rapid transition, was alive at this time.) The book closes with the observation — more cynical, one suspects, than its author realized — made by Captain Blathers, 'with a characteristic oath, that he had not much opinion of religion in his own country, but he was bound to say it was "a first-rate institootion in the South Seas" '.[64]

In W. H. G. Kingston's twenty odd novels set in the Pacific standards of conduct are no less imperialist and genteel, but the tone is more optimistic and genial. There is less punishment of the heathen, more confidence in their eventual conversion; and one of Kingston's aims is the moral rescue of the fallen whites. Mary the missionary's daughter persuades a young English pleasure-seeker to turn missionary. Little Ben Hadden (the subtitle of his story is 'Do Right Whatever Comes of It') rescues a long-lost brother living as a beachcomber on an island like Angatan, and follows up with an action neglected by James Bowman: he arranges for a missionary to be sent there.[65]

But the emphasis is on the contrast between the condition of islanders before and after conversion. In *Round the World* two boys temporarily marooned on an uninhabited island are visited, not by heathen savages, but by Polynesian missionaries who, like Bowman's Eiulo, show their skills by repairing their canoe, giving the boys the best food and serving them first. Christian villages of neat whitewashed cottages in rows are contrasted with the disorderly heathen villages (though in fact the historian of missions Niel Gunson tells us that quite early the Tahitians had given up living in the partitioned cottages).[66] A captain impressed by the shirts and trousers and orderly behaviour of the natives of one of the Society Islands remarks on the changes since his last visit. He is told: 'We were then heathen savages; we are now Christian men.' What emigration could do for Chartists, conversion could do for Pacific islanders. It is through Mary Liddiard's friend Lisele, ripe for conversion like Bowman's Angatau chief's wife, that her father is converted, and so the whole island. And even the fierce old Typee chief, borrowed from Melville, takes a protective interest in the boy heroes, and though the heathen Typees win a battle, Motakee goes against his people, like Bowman's Wakatta, in coming to the ship to see the boys leave. All the same, the heathens have to be controlled or outwitted. In *Peter Trawl* a captain passing Kusaie, one of the Caroline Islands, fires a nine-pounder 'to show them that we're wide awake' because the king is unable to control his people. In *Old Jack*, a boy who is alone on a coral island in the Fiji group believes that savage people look on madmen as sacred, and puts on an act, salaaming and bowing, leaping about and clapping his hands and shouting meaningless exclamations (one of them Irish) — using an excessive servility and frivolity that are simply the reverse of the manly virtues Kingston favoured. The ruse works, and Jack is able to paddle off in the full view of his captors.[67]

The attitude of a later writer for boys George Manville Fenn is more repulsive, since it is without the geniality or the moral concern of the Christian writers. Fenn's contempt is not only for all forms of superstition, Christian or heathen, but for all blacks, domesticated or wild. It is a rationalist version of Ballantyne's white supremacy and its baldest assertions of inherent racial differences in intelligence carry the false authority of being uttered by characters who are scientists.

The territory of contemporary literary savages by the end of the century has moved to New Guinea, and in Fenn's *Nat the Naturalist* (1899), in which the heroes' naturalism consists of shooting birds to take them home as scientific specimens, they are enabled to escape from the armed and fierce New Guinea men by the help of a tame black man who volunteered as their Friday; and they think it sufficient to reward him with trade goods. In *Bunyip Land* (1885) a botanist says it is degrading to have to rely on a savage, whose mentality is that of an English boy of nine or ten. In *King o' the Beach* (1899) a boy indulges a contempt for the wild New Guinean who serves him like a dog, whose loyalty is won by being harsh. It is the unanimous view of the adults in this novel that the harder you are, the more blacks will respect you. This boy's habit is to rap Jackum on the knuckles with an iron spoon. When the time comes to leave, the only way he can shake Jackum off is to tell him to go on collecting copra, shell, and pearls for him until he comes back, though he knows he isn't likely to.

There were eighteen or so serious writers of imperialist fiction for boys, and up to 1923, fifty-eight titles had been published, set in the Pacific islands. Some nineteenth-century titles were re-published or reprinted in the twentieth century, and four of the writers first appeared in the twentieth century. Much of it was available when I was a boy in the nineteen-twenties and thirties, in school libraries or given as school prizes. So that for a period of sixty years or more there was this body of reading encouraging boys of Britain and the Dominions to racial arrogance. Even though it was stated in most novels that the events had occurred many years earlier, one wonders to what extent they retarded the development of the attitudes necessary for decolonization. It is notable that these books were seldom published in the United States and there is no exact equivalent in American publishing. But there is a counterpart, and that is the dime novels and their successors published by the firm of Beadle and Adams between 1860 and 1897. In the first twenty years of this series the greatest number is concerned with the American west, and the fierce enemy of course is the Red Indian, but he is more often killed than domesticated.

3
VIEWS FROM THE BEACH

In 1829 a tale by Jane Porter appeared in a Sydney newspaper, presumably reprinted from an English source, recognizably based on the experience of the French beachcomber Jean Cabri (or Joseph Kabris), who spent eight years on the Marquesas. He had identified himself so closely with the culture of his hosts that he was tattooed from the calves of his legs to his forehead, and had almost forgotten his language and his born name. He had married and had some chiefly status. He had taken part in war and was adept with the slingstone in the hunting of victims for sacrifice; he told the Russian navigator Langsdorff that he traded them for pigs.[1] It was by mishap and unwillingly that he went in the Russian ship, which landed him at Kamchatka. Jane Porter's brother, the painter Robert Ker Porter, met him at Moscow where he sought help to return to the Marquesas. He had become adept enough in recrossing the cultural beach, to use Greg Dening's metaphor, to present his plight in sentimental and heroic terms that might appeal to his European listeners.[2] In fact he had to end his days performing dances and displaying his tattoos at country fairs in France. Jane Porter relocates him on Tahiti and gives his wife the name of Oberea, slightly changed. The fantasy she invents is familiar, but it is based on what Cabri told her brother, who saw in Cabri's story 'grounds for a very pretty romance'. In her tale the daughter of a chief fell in love with him, the King invested him with the highest order of Tahitian nobility and made him his regent. By means of his firearms he eliminated cannibalism and he acted as pilot for visiting European vessels. He was an agent of civilization.

Jane Porter presents her character's plight in terms both genteel and sentimental, in the rhetoric of the Gothic novel already used in the phrases of Robert Porter from which she rewrote this passage: ' "I was then beloved," said he, "Honoured! — Master of all around me. Now, I am nothing: — no home — no wife — no friend! I am an outcast here! — when there! Oh Berea! Wilt thou have forgotten me?" His tears, and wild agonies, prevented him proceeding; and my eyes could not remain dry, when seeing such genuine grief, such real suffering.' Miss Porter sees to it that, in her tale at least, he finds a boat home.[3]

In spite of the sentimentalization, some of the elements of his situation are recognizably like those of actual Pacific beachcombers who have left records of their experiences. Cabri's own account, dictated and recently published in translation, is not very revealing of his personal experience.[4] But the accounts of other beachcombers are. H. E. Maude has pointed out their unique value as a source of knowledge for historians and anthropologists, and if one looks at them in literary terms they have the value of a credible lifelikeness or the impression of actual experience, so rare in the writing I have already discussed. The writers of these accounts were valued by the chiefs for their versatility in European technical skills, including warfare; and they were usually given chiefly status, often by the Polynesian device of name exchange which made them kin of the chief's family, with an immediate set of rights and obligations. They differed from the seamen visitors in several essential ways that Maude describes: 'They treated the islanders with friendship and respect as equals, and their chiefs with the courtesy due to their rank, while taking great pains to avoid any conduct that might outrage the local norms of behaviour; equally important, they readily assisted them with firearms in attacking their neighbours.' They were incidentally as much agents of acculturation as the missionaries, though in the eyes of the missionaries and visiting captains they were renegades, vile and degraded. Maude puts it another way: they were 'often drunken, profligate and quarrelsome, but still essentially human and tolerant, and wishing to change no one.'[5]

Their experience as told in their memoirs is very different from the censorious conception of it in Tennyson's widely read poem 'Locksley Hall', published in 1842 but written four or five years earlier. In this poem the protagonist, unhappy at the stress of living in times of progress, wishes for an easy life on one of the 'summer isles of Eden', married to a 'savage woman' and parent to a dusky race of 'gray barbarians', pagan and lithe among a people of low intelligence and animal pleasures. The woman is described as a 'squalid savage' — 'steept perhaps in savage crime' a manuscript draft adds; and the protagonist rejects the temptation as unworthy of one who knows he is

> The heir of all the ages, in the foremost files of time.

One notes how narrow is Tennyson's conception of the beachcomber life as an irresponsible Crusoe existence without other relationships than to wife and children, apparently sons. The virtue is entirely with Europe:

> Better fifty years of Europe than a cycle of Cathay![6]

Tennyson, however, is addressing himself less to any knowledge of beachcomber experience than to a simple theoretical contrast between a mentally sluggish 'natural' existence and the challenge of life in nineteenth-century England.

It is their biculturalism or their ability to walk on the borders of both cultures that makes the experience of actual beachcombers more interesting than this or the vicarious fiction I have already described, and it is their human sympathy that enables them to cross the beach. This humanity involves not only their sympathy for their hosts; it also involves an ambivalence or watchfulness that comes from their attachment to values of their own culture. That seems to underlie their lack of compunction in killing islanders who were at enmity, or the repeated instances of their confessing to visiting captains that they distrusted and even disliked the people they were living with, or their asking for a passage home.

There is a notable instance of a cultural encounter in Melville's *Typee*, where in 1842 Melville and his friend Toby Green are weighed up by the chiefs of the Taipi clan:

> Close to where we lay, squatting upon their haunches, were some eight or ten noble-looking chiefs — for such they subsequently proved to be — who, more reserved than the rest, regarded us with a fixed and stern attention, which not a little discomposed our equanimity. One of them in particular, who appeared to be the highest in rank, placed himself directly facing me; looking at me with a rigidity of aspect under which I absolutely quailed. He never once opened his lips, but maintained his severe expression of countenance, without turning his face aside for a single moment. Never before had I been subjected to so strange and steady a glance; it revealed nothing of the mind of the savage, but it appeared to be reading my own.
> After undergoing this scrutiny till I grew absolutely nervous, with a view of diverting it if possible, and conciliating the good opinion of the warrior, I took some tobacco from the bosom of my frock and offered it to him. He quietly rejected the proffered gift, and, without speaking, motioned me to return it to its place.[7]

It is a confrontation between Polynesian chiefly authority and the conventions of the casual egalitarianism of the frontiersman. Melville goes on to say that among the other inhabitants of Nukuhiva, the Teii and the Taioa, who had been used to visitors for fifty years, a gift of tobacco would have been a passport to acceptance.

Edward Robarts, coming ashore for the first time on Tahuata in 1798, had a different introduction, this time to Polynesian hospitality to guests, or to Marquesan polyandry:

> I must here beg leave of my fair reader to permit me to relate such matters of fact as are within bounds. My friend took me by the hand and led me to the side of his consort who was sitting on a fine matt. I was a little surpriz'd at this part of the cerimony when he told me I must sleep on the same matt with her. I must confess the ladys artillery was powerfull enough for any man to surrender, but I could not accept of this unrivaled peice of friendship. I ashurd him by sighns that I was perfectly satisfied of his sincear friendship towards me and begd leave to retire at a becomeing distance from his consort, which was granted. I told him it was against the laws of my country to sleep with other mens wives. He then insisted I should have a companion that was not married.[8]

Robarts spent seven years in the Marquesas; because of his skills he was sought after, and became the son-in-law of the powerful chief Keatonui and the adopted son of every great chief on three islands. By his tapu status and his qualities as a commander in war he survived those seven years until an intrigue within his father-in-law's family caused him to leave rather than 'lift my hand against my relations'. In that statement of principle his adherence to the loyalties of his own culture is notable. His repeated gallantries to the ladies were subversive to the proprieties of his host's culture. He frequently ate with them, asking that food be not placed on a tapu place; his wife seems to have eaten pork with him. I am not as convinced as his editor that his consciousness of himself as a protector of the weak and as a gallant with the ladies belongs more to his literary medium than to himself. Certainly his prose is full of the cliches of the language of sentiment, with silent tears of gratitude, addresses to 'my fair reader' and a disclaimer of 'ungenerous, unmanly thoughts'. But his sense of fairness leads him to restore on his own initiative to his father-in-law's sister the land of which she had been dispossessed by some warriors. And once, leading his party of warriors in battle, and having his enemies on the run, he comes across a group of women deserted by the fleeing men, trembling and 'expecting every moment to be torn to pieces.' He stops his party from proceeding further.

When I came up to the women, I stuck my spear in the ground with my turban hung to it, as no one would pass my spear with my turban hung to it. I told the poor women not to be frightend. Not one of them should be hurt. They set down. My men I Kept back and told them it was unbecomeing a brave man to hurt a woman. With reluctance they obeyd.

Some of these women he already knows; they include 'several fine, handsome, young ladies, daughters of Chieftains among them'. He sat a while and talked with them before ordering a general retreat.

He confesses he is amazed by a contradiction: 'I have often been amazed with these people, to experience their hospitality and see their Kindness one among another, and yet in their wars they have no mercy. If a grown girl or young child is taken, Beauty or the tears of the infant has no effect on them'. His cultural bafflement is so precisely defined that it is equally amazing that he did not see that he had gone some way to answering his question when he says '[it was] only on account of the Fair sex being in the way [that the enemy were spared]. [Otherwise] I would not have spared a man of them.' My point is that there is comparable discrepancy in his own behaviour in peace and war, though its boundaries are defined differently.[9]

Like Cabri, Robarts laments his loss of power when he leaves Nukuhiva. 'I could not but regret that but the day before I was a great man, and now look at myself — the outcast of fortune, an unfortunate stranger going to a strange land without money and without friends.'[10]

In Tahiti he turns to distilling rum and finds himself having to outwit a cunning and alcoholic King; when the King gets possession of the still, Robarts puts it out of action. The ease with which he related to Marquesan society does not prevent him falling into fierce hostility towards the peoples of a Tuamotuan island and of New Ireland; and our last knowledge of this former Marquesan chief is as a police constable in Calcutta. His few years of greatness resulted from a coincidence of scope for his powers in a culture his very presence was subtly changing.

I have already mentioned William Mariner's experience of the natives of the Tonga Islands, scrupulously written by John Martin, published in 1817, translated into French, and into a third edition by 1827. It was deservedly widely read in its day and one can see reflections of the book not only in Byron and Sarah Ellis but in a number of lesser writers.

Mariner was four years in Tonga, involuntarily saved from a massacre of the ship's crew because Finau Ulukalala liked him and adopted him as a son. A dispensation to avoid local mandates because of attachment to his own principles, was allowed him, for example, when he asked to be excused Finau's request to shoot an insane woman at Lifuka; 'assuring the king that he was perfectly willing to risk his life in his service against his enemies; but that it was quite contrary to the sentiment of the religion in which he had been brought up, and to the laws of his country, to destroy an innocent fellow creature in cold blood.'[11]

In a short time he learned the language and became a chief and military commander, so well acquainted with affairs of state and the customs of the country as to provide the material for John Martin's detailed and systematic account of them, still relied on by ethnographers. Mariner was assigned an adoptive mother, one of Finau's wives, who remembered him well enough to write to him many years later in a language he had by that time forgotten, when he was employed as a stockbroker in the City of London.[12] Mariner's uprightness and his generosity of spirit are notable. There is one example in his appreciative description of the chief, Hala Api Api, a description which perhaps reflects Martin's reading of Walter Scott: 'a slim yet athletic and active figure, of a middling stature, full of fire and impetuosity; endowed with a mind replete with the most romantic notions of heroic bravery: full of mischief (without malignity), wrought up with the most exuberant generosity: the heat and inconstancy of youth was in him strangely mixed with the steadiness and wisdom of age'. There is a recognition of distinctive personal qualities not apparent in the missionary derived writing. And about the same man, there is a passage that concerns him as a champion of the oppressed, and also concerns Polynesian volatility, or fullness of feeling.

> He would weep at the distress of which they complained, and the next moment his eyes would flash with indignation, at the injustice of the oppressor, and seizing his club, he would sally forth to redress their wrongs. . . . Talk to him about battles, and he looked as if he were inspired. Tell him a pathetic story, and the tears would run down his cheeks faster than you could count them. Tell him a good joke, and there was nobody would laugh more heartily than he.'[13]

It is a generous response to a quality that Mrs Ellis had belittled. She was writing at second hand, but perhaps was at no further remove from a first-hand source, her husband, than Martin was from Mariner.

Warm and impetuous natures, born to feel
Each impulse of the moment — burning zeal
One hour, and languid thought the next,
Changing their purpose with each new pretext.[14]

Perhaps this passage is what she remembered of the passage in Mariner.

A far less admirable figure is William Diaper (or Diapea), living by his wits and his musket and a versatility in skills in Vanua Levu and several islands in the Lau group and Tonga in the eighteen-forties. Boasted father of thirty-eight children and ninety-nine grandchildren, a man of status and privilege, with three wives in Fiji, mending muskets for his chief and amassing property, his adventures are usually free of attachment to other principles than a circumspect self interest. Yet there are revelations of his humanity and perception of it in others that make his account of himself interesting. He pleads for the life of a destined victim and finds to his surprise that the chief himself is relieved to be freed of the obligation to kill the man, and in turn when destined himself for torture and death at the hands of enemies, he is released by the man whose life he had saved. The same man prevents Diaper's three wives from immolating themselves when he is absent on a trading expedition for too long.

There are incidents of no less wonder, that a writer of great talent could have made much of. A chief Finau (of a later generation than those of the same name in Mariner) impatient with being ill, fills his house with coconut leaves and other combustibles, and burns himself to death with his canoe. Diaper sails to Tonga on a double canoe through a fierce storm which drowns all the crew and breaks up the canoe. He has lashed himself to the deck and is so discovered washed up on the shore of an island in the Lau group, by a chief's daughter Litia, who finds him a spot under a banyan tree and nurses him back to health. She fears that her father would kill him if she took him home as a victim of shipwreck, but she knows he would be acceptable as a casual lover brought home from a visiting ship, and so they deceive her father. When Diaper is due to leave on the ship, she refuses to be separated from him, threatens suicide, and a youth to whom she is contracted resigns her to him. There are mutual harassments between Christian followers of her father and pagans who are led by her uncle. Diaper shoots her uncle dead, and her Christian father sets fire to the temple in which the pagans have taken refuge and they are tomahawked as they leave. Some widows strangle themselves, and two little girls have to be dragged from the graves in which their parents are buried.[15]

I am reciting without comment this series of incidents to illustrate a likeness of the raw material of much of the literature. With a different bias they could have been told by the early missionary writers, and at the same time each incident reads like a tale of Louis Becke, without his attempt at emotional effect.

On Vava'u and Niuafo'ou Diaper gets the better of some swaggering louts — 'larrikins' he calls them — who tease him violently, by a combination of superior cunning and force or the threat of his musket.

There is a comic incident of a court which sits in judgement on a couple who have offended sexually against missionary laws. The judge promises leniency if the lady will forget the shame and tell every detail including the identity of all she has been with. The courts and the judge cheer at the revelations. Diaper has become a successful pig-breeder and provisioner of ships, he caters for picnics for visiting officers, mends books at a profit of 1000 per cent — 'about fifty irons in the fire at once, and not one of them burnt'. But this man of three wives in Fiji cannot get one here because the Tongan women disdain foreigners and in desperation he runs about scattering in handfuls the money that will not attract a wife.

Diaper's entire journal has never been published. I do not know if he returned to England. He died an old man on Maré, one of the Loyalty Islands.

The best known of the beachcomber narratives, and the most rewarding as literature, are of course Melville's *Typee* and *Omoo*. In the light of the beachcomber books I have mentioned, *Typee* has more in common with the accounts of the eighteenth-century navigators in that Melville's visit was short, he didn't speak the language, and he saw the people in a state of excitation caused by his very presence. He himself was in a state of excitation caused by his anxiety to escape, and he was in constant fear of the fickleness of the 'savages'. His very conclusions on the relation between the Marquesans and the civilized world are to some extent the same as those of the Forsters.

The facts of Melville's visit to Nukuhiva, and the use he made of printed sources, have been known for forty years or more, thanks to the research of R. S. Forsythe and C. R. Anderson confirming the essential truth of his account. That truth was challenged by some reviewers and was the only doubt about *Typee* entertained by the English publisher,

John Murray — the publisher, incidentally, of Mariner and of Byron. The American publisher objected to the passages that offended supporters of missions. In fact many of the passages for which *Typee* is famous, those that favourably compare Taipi life with civilization, were not available to the American reading public for thirty years from the issue of the revised edition in 1846. Fortunately the English edition continued to be issued unrevised.[16]

Melville was on Nukuhiva for less than four weeks, and in his account of the behaviour of Taipi his own observations are supplemented by borrowings from the published accounts of the Russian navigator Langsdorff (on Nukuhiva in 1804), the American captain David Porter (there in 1813), and the American naval chaplain C. S. Stewart (there in 1831). Since the most of the information given by these writers was obtained from beachcombers — from Cabri and Robarts in the case of Langsdorff — it is generally reliable, and one can see that Melville has gone to them in search of further understanding of what he saw himself, and has wisely omitted explanations. But he raises uncomfortable questions that they did not, not only the not unusual comparison of the worth of the simple life and civilization, but questions about replacing a palpably attractive society with an unattractive travesty of civilization. Melville's pleasant impression of life in the Taipivai valley is confirmed both by Langsdorff and by Stewart, who said it only needed missionary instruction to turn the nearby valley of the Taioa morally and spiritually into 'the happy valley'.[17] David Porter too has some praise for the Nukuhivans even if it is offset by the destructive events which Melville deplored, when in a mood of chauvinist pique Porter laid waste the settlements of the Taipi.[18] Melville refers twice to that atrocity and there is a recurring anxiety in *Typee* that the happiness of the valley is threatened, following the French annexation that occurred between Melville's two visits to the island.

What is unusual in Melville is the genial sympathy with the people of the valley as fellow humans with motives and feelings like his own. It is not special pleading but an egalitarian sense of justice that caused him to write: 'They seemed to be governed by that sort of tacit common-sense law which, say what they will of the inborn lawlessness of the human race, has its precepts graven on every breast. The grand principles of virtue and honor, however they may be distorted by arbitrary codes, are the same all the world over: and where these principles are concerned, the right or wrong of any action appears the same to the uncultivated as to the enlightened mind.' [19] It is especially on this point that Melville's attitude differs from that of the Forsters: there is no patronage or paternalism. The frontiersman's egalitarianism takes in the people on the other side of the frontier.

One trusts Melville's descriptions. It is not surprising to find him quoted on Marquesan stone structures in a standard work of Marquesan ethnography and another on Pacific prehistory. I find both entertaining and trustworthy his descriptions of Taipi religious ceremony, because his sceptical bias is implied in his genial style. It contrasts with other presentations of religion. In the writers who draw on missionary sources heathen priests are always sinister. Even in Robarts the *tau'a*, in his seizure of inspiration, is described as 'this Pagan deluder ... who set rocking from side to side like a greenland bear adrift on a peice of ice' speaking 'with a shrill squeaking voice, prophecying many things that never came to pass.' [20]

To Melville the priests were 'the merriest dogs of the valley' and the ceremony he observes in which the priest he calls 'Kolory' communicates in a spirit of apparently irreverent familiarity with an effigy of a god, is entertaining but not belittling. There is a humble admission that though there was hardly a day that he didn't witness some religious ceremony or other, he did not understand it: 'I saw everything, but could comprehend nothing.' [21] For this reason I trust his account of the esoteric ceremony to which he was not admitted, which he suspected was, and leads the reader to believe was, a sacramental eating of human flesh by the senior men.

There is, however, the usual beachcomber's ambivalence in Melville. One reason for it is his fear of the reputation for cannibalism of the Taipi, whom he and Toby Green hadn't intended to visit anyway. And though he does not say how long they planned to stay on the island, there is no reason to believe they intended to stay long. Greg Dening tells us that before Melville there had been 150 beachcombers on the Marquesas, some of whom stayed only a few days, like Toby Green, till the next ship called. Tommo and Toby became alarmed at the unexpectedly high value that was set on them and at their hosts' watchfulness. Tommo, with an injured leg and Toby mysteriously gone, unable to communicate fully or freely with anyone, felt captive. The framework of *Typee* is in fact that of a captivity narrative, but its core, instead of a recital of cruelties, privations, and repulsive food, is an idyll of favoured treatment, admirable customs and good food. The motif of escape, however, is not forgotten for long. It comes up when Toby goes to the coast and doesn't return; it isn't dropped till the eighteenth chapter — more than half-way through the book — when Tommo learns how angry the chiefs are at his desire to leave. It is forgotten for the twelve chapters of pleasant description of Marquesan life, but it is reintroduced five chapters before the end, when three incidents revive Tommo's impatience to get away. There is the chief's desire that he should be tattooed — which we can assume (if Tommo didn't) would have been an emblem of his reception into the chiefly class, and would have guaranteed his safety except in war — and there is the suspected cannibal ritual. Then 'Marnoo' the visitor from the other bay warns him that if he does not stay with the chiefs they might kill him. The escape itself is told in some of the sensational cliches of the captivity narrative. On the last page the Taipi once again become 'savages' and 'infuriated wretches'. The cliches surround his last hostile act when 'with a true aim' Tommo 'exert[s] all his strength' as he 'dashes' the boat-hook at the throat of the one-eyed chief 'Mow Mow' and kills him. Melville's biographer Leon Howard is sceptical of this incident. Tommo, we recall, runs through the surf to a waiting boat which pulls out of the the reach of his captors. However 'Mow Mow' and thirty others run to the point of a headland to intercept the boat and swim out to it. With the geography of Comptroller's Bay in mind, Howard has pointed out that they would have had to run for a mile along a coast of rocky cliffs rising straight out from the sea that had kept the Taipi and Hapa'a clans separate for generations. But, even though the geography of the bay doesn't leave much room for manoeuvre, we can't know how close to actuality Melville is intending to be. What is suggested however by the placing of this hostile last act of Tommo's towards the very hosts of whom Melville wrote so affectionately is the helplessness of an individual westerner, in such a situation, to avoid the very evil that Tommo deplores, the destruction of the integrity of the happy valley.

It was Tommo who put himself in the situation in the first place. Though Melville does not expand on the incident of the boat-hook and it is presented as little more than the decisive act by which Tommo escaped, I suspect that it implies a recognition of a contradiction in even sympathetic contact with the islanders' life.

I don't believe those essays in the critical journals that have treated *Typee* as a rejection of Eden or repudiation of the 'noble savage'. I have found helpful a book that included *Typee* along with other works of Melville in a study of the treatment of American Indians in American literature.[22] Melville's concern for the victims of western expansion is consistent and in the Taipivai valley he has found a people exempt from the demoralization to which the Hawaiians and Tahitians had been brought. But he is aware that it is only for a time. He predicts that following French annexation 'all peace and happiness' will have been driven from the valley in a few years: he foresees an onset of disease and death, followed by European expropriation, settlement, and neat little suburbs. In a public lecture reported in a Baltimore newspaper in 1859 he reasserted his belief in the sense of fair-dealing in the Pacific Islanders and his opposition to western annexation.[23] If he argues in *Typee*, 'let the savages be civilized, but civilize them with benefits and not with evils', that was the sort of reflex pious wish anyone might come up with. He is no more convinced than George Forster that it is likely. In his imaginative conviction that conflict between the authority of the Taipi chiefs and the egalitarianism of the frontier is decided by history in favour of the expanding frontier, the dispossessed join an international community of seamen and take up their moral positions as reliable comrades like Queequeg or agents of the oppressor like Bembo or Tashtego.

What of the alterations Melville made? The most notable is his relationship with Fayaway. It could hardly have been other than a full Polynesian marriage, but all we can believe of Melville's presentation of it is Fayaway's violent, indignant sobs as he leaves her. It must have been his sense of the puritanism of the American reading public that caused him to be so reticent, and to present the affair so sentimentally. The episode of sailing with her on the lake is artificial: a sketch made from a photograph shows some widening of the river near the mouth, behind a spit, but there is no lake; and it is scarcely credible that the priests could be persuaded to relax the tapu against women being in canoes in the interest of a convention of romantic courtship foreign to them.[24] This incident in which Fayaway standing upright, disrobes and uses her mantle as a sail, is a charming conceit, a triumph as a sailor's yarn whose sentimental charm conceals its affront to puritanism.

Before I leave Melville there is a famous comment on *Typee* I want to elucidate because I think it is misleading. It is from D. H. Lawrence's *Studies in Classic American Literature*. It has geological layers that involve a change in Lawrence's position, and I think Lawrence's central point is irrelevant to Melville.

First, the most recent layer. From the 1923 version of his essay, I take two extracts:

The Maoris, the Tongans, the Marquesans, the Fijians, the Polynesians: holy

God, how long have they been turning over in the same sleep, with varying dreams? . . .
    Samoa, Tahiti, Raratonga, Nukuheva: the very names are a sleep and a forgetting. . . .²⁵

If one didn't pick up the reference to Wordsworth one could take this as an impatient dismissal of the tourist myth of the South Seas, the summer isles of Eden of Charles Warren Stoddard and H. Stonehewer Cooper and Edward O'Brien, a myth which Lawrence himself shared to the extent of reporting that Rarotonga in 1922 was 'almost as lovely as one expects these South Sea Islands to be'.* ²⁶ But this third version of Lawrence's essay incorporates his spleen against Mabel Dodge Luhan, the lady who had first persuaded him to leave Sicily and come to Taos, New Mexico. She was a former New York socialite and divorcee who had married an American Indian, Tony Luhan, and took a patronizing interest in the local Apaches. She talked close-to-the-earth simplicity for them, while living expensively herself. Lawrence quickly became revolted by the falsity of her position; and his anger touched his earlier reaction to Melville, exposing I believe an earlier misunderstanding. His best-known statement was made after this disillusionment in Taos:

    The truth of the matter is, one cannot go back. Some men can: renegade. But Melville couldn't go back . . . and I know now that I could never go back. Back towards the past, savage life. . . . We can only do it when we are renegade. The renegade hates life itself. He wants the death of life. So these many 'reformers' and 'idealists' who glorify the savages in America. They are death-birds, life-haters. Renegades.²⁷

He clearly has Mrs Luhan in mind, but 'renegade' is what the missionaries called the early beachcombers. There is a strange likeness in Lawrence's position, as he expressed it here, to that of Southey and the contributors to the *Anti-Jacobin* and the *Quarterly Review* to those who eulogized Tahiti. Mrs Luhan has caused him to think again about himself and about Melville; and it is necessary to go back at least to his earlier

---

* It was after the disappointment of false expectations that Lawrence turned against the myth a few days later following a visit to Papeʻete. (The reaction is mixed with a groundswell of subjective reaction to the tropics in general that must have begun in Ceylon.) 'Papeete is a poor sort of place, mostly Chinese, natives in European clothes, and fat. We motored out — again beautiful to look at, but I never want to *stay* in the tropics. There is a sort of sickliness about them, smell of cocoa-nut oil and sort of palm-tree, reptile nausea. But lovely flowers, especially Rarotonga. These are supposed to be the earthly paradises: these South Sea Isles. You can have 'em.'

version of the essay, written in Sicily in 1920, to see what he meant by 'a sleep and a forgetting' and by 'going back'. In that earlier essay his enthusiasm for Melville and for the Marquesans is warmer, and he proposed a theory of an ancient vast Pacific civilization that included China, Japan, Mexico and Peru, and Polynesia, which existed 'before the geological cataclysms,' whatever they were. It was a 'sensual-mystic' civilization and its principle was spontaneity, and it is completely inaccessible to our civilization, whose principle is self-consciousness. It is inaccessible too to existing Pacific peoples who can only experience dreams of it, and their modern life is a garbling of truths they no longer understand. 'They are old, grotesque people, dreaming over their once wide-awake realities.' Here is the earlier version of the passage I have quoted. It is that rather than Melville that Lawrence has reacted against:

> At the very centre of the old primeval world sleeps the living and forgetting of the South Sea Isles, Samoa, Tahiti, Nukuheva, places with the magic names. Wordsworth hints at the sleep-forgotten past magnificence of human history in his 'trailing clouds of glory do we come'. Tahiti, Samoa, Nukuheva, the very names are clouds of glory. They are echoes from the world once splendid in the fulness of the other way of knowledge.[28]

And in this essay Lawrence writes of Melville's Taipi as being 'good and gentle' and their life as 'refined and concentrated, and self-understood to a degree that makes our life laughably crude.' Lawrence even appears to pity Melville for being unable to make contact with their 'subtle . . . non-mental understanding,' their spontaneous rapport.

In the revised essay it is a point in Melville's favour that he was unable to make contact. And now the phrase is 'going back' — the model has changed: not a model of an inaccessible civilization based on a different mode of knowledge, inaccessible across a gulf of time, but a linear model of simple evolutionary progression and nothing completely forgotten. Lawrence expresses it in another essay written at about the same time, after attending an Apache festival. In this essay he claims that he already knows all that primitive man can teach him, it is already incorporated in him. 'But me, the conscious me, I have gone a long road since then. . . . But there is no going back. Always onward, still further. The great devious onward-flowing stream of conscious human blood. From them to me, and from me on.' [29]

There is a strangely mid-Victorian ring about this in spite of the irrationality. But Lawrence has missed one aspect of *Typee*, that however attractive Melville made the people of the valley, he didn't want their life for himself. There is no justification for thinking that he intended to stay for long and it is unlikely he would have wanted to even without his fears of being kept a favoured prisoner.

The literary treatment of Pacific island young women is usually one of subjection. Benjamin Morrell has a passage of eloquent, imaginatively tactile, lust on the nubility of two girls on Nomoi, in the Carolines.

> ... and as if this had been a preconcerted signal, two lovely females, naked as they were born, darted from a neighbouring thicket, each with a similar token of affection, which they offered with the most bewitching grace conceivable. Heaven forgive me, if my wicked heart did violence to any one precept of the decalogue!
> These girls were about sixteen or seventeen, with eyes like the gazelle's, teeth like ivory, and the most delicately formed features I have ever met with. In stature they were about five feet, with small hands, feet and head, long black hair, and then those eyes, sparkling like jet beads, swimming in liquid enamel! They had plump cheeks, with a chin to match, and lips of just the proper thickness for affection's kiss. Their necks were small, and I believe that I could have spanned either of their naked waists with both my hands. Their limbs were beautifully proportioned and so were their busts. Imagination must complete the bewitching portraits: I will only add the shade — their skin was a light copper colour.

And whether he set foot on Truk or not, he had indulged himself in this description of the Trukese women in exclusively erotic terms:

> The women are small in size, with very handsome delicate features, and a dark sparkling eye, expressive of tenderness and affection. They have round luxuriant chests, slender waists, small hands and feet, straight legs and small ankles. In short, they are seen to be, in every respect, admirably 'fitted for the tender offices of love;' and, setting aside our innate prejudice to certain complexions, their personal charms are of a very superior order.[30]

More genteel but, I think, more open to objection is the attitude expressed in a novel written by Dora Hort, the wife of a merchant in Pape'ete. Published in 1866, titled *Hena, or Life in Tahiti*, the story opens with two young white men, English and French, watching two girls bathing. One of them is Hena, a half-caste, barely fourteen, and though neither knows it, she is half-sister to the Frenchman who is admiring her since his father had sown wild oats as a young naval officer. Although Hena has been brought up by Tahitians, she is afraid of that part of her ancestry, fearing that she might be as promiscuous as her mother. The assumption that fickleness is in the blood is illustrated in an inset story in which a lively girl keeps deceiving her husband in his absence, and in a mood of contrition, says ' "... I have acted like a thorough native, as I am" '. Hena will not entertain the attentions of a young chief of unmixed ancestry, saying ' "I am dark enough myself, without marrying one darker." ' She falls in love with the young Englishman, who discourages her, but 'a native woman or girl conceives herself the better loved when thus maltreated' and so she loves him the more. 'Here her native blood showed itself: she would rather have been his slave than anybody else's wife, for his sake she would have submitted to any degradation, without an after regret'.[31] When she sees a miniature of Seymour's fiancée, she falls into a fever. Nevertheless Seymour does marry Hena, and for a while forbids her to associate with Tahitians, even her adoptive family, though he later relents. Her illness is progressive and before she dies she tells a young English woman Mary that 'Mr Seymour' deserves a wife more accomplished than she. She asks Mary to wear her wedding-ring when she dies and to name her first baby girl after her. Since in fact Mary becomes Seymour's next wife, this is a myth of renunciation. Mrs Hort repeats the story with altered names thirty years later in a novel called *Tiari* (1893) in which before the heroine dies with her head against her husband's breast, he says ' "Oh, my darling, darling wife, to me you will ever be a sweet memory." '[32]

Mrs Hort seems to have anticipated the famous French romance *Rarahu* or *The Marriage of Loti*, in which a young English officer first sees his beloved bathing with a friend in a stream. *Rarahu* was first published in 1880, and according to the recent translation by Wright and Eleanor Frierson which I am using, it had reached 211 editions by 1926. This is the one nineteenth-century French work that I am considering, and I am doing so because it embodies a type situation. It is a sentimental story about a Tahitian fourteen-year-old who dies young. Certainly it is pathetic, tender, exquisite, delicately written, but like many sentimental situations it disguises a contradiction — an objectionably exploitative attitude.

The author, Julien Viaud, who took the pen name of Pierre Loti, had called at Pape'ete as a young naval officer, twice in 1872; at first for a period of just under eight weeks, then for a period of nine or ten days. In *Rarahu* he imagines an affair that lasts several months between a young English officer and a fourteen-year-old, whom he says he created from several real people, as a faithful enough portrait of the young Tahitian woman. The romance is a notebook of moments in their idyllic affair, which has become no more than an exquisite memory.

As 'the little wife of Loti' Rarahu has been artless, child-like, devoted. When he attends royal functions from which she is excluded she stands outside watching him enjoying himself without her. But he is always aware of the distance between them, they talk in 'the Tahitian of the beach', he notices 'her cannibal teeth'. 'She was a little savage; between us who had become one flesh remained the radical distinction of race, the divergence of elementary concepts about all things'. 'It is not possible for us who were born on the other side of the world to judge or even to comprehend these incomplete natures so different from ours, whose souls remain mysterious and savage but where one can still find, at certain times, so much of the charm of love and of exquisite sensibility.' And he knows that when he leaves, she will again become 'a little Maori [i.e. Polynesian] girl, ignorant and savage.'[33]

There is one revealing scene. They are returning to their hut after they have been separated each having different functions to perform during a royal visit to Mo'orea. At a procession at Afareaitu he had partnered the princess. This incident follows:

> I was expecting a scene, reproaches, and tears. Instead of all that, she smiled while turning away her head with an almost imperceptible movement of the shoulders, an unexpected expression of disenchantment, of bitter sadness and irony.
> That smile and that gesture said as much as a very long discourse; they were saying in a concise and striking way something like this:
> I knew very well that I was only an inferior little creature, a chance plaything that you have given yourself. For you people, white men, that's all we are able to be. But what good would it do me to be angry about it? I am alone in the world; to belong to you or to another, what does it matter? I was your mistress; here was our dwelling; I know that you desire me still. So, I stay and here I am.
> The unsophisticated little girl had made terrible strides in knowledge of the facts of life. The savage child had become stronger than her master and dominated him.
> I regarded her in silence, with surprise and sorrow; I felt an immense pity for her. And it was I who asked forgiveness, nearly in tears and covering her with kisses.
> She loved me still, yes, as one might love a supernatural being that one could scarcely apprehend or understand. Sweet and peaceful days of love once again succeeded the experience of Afareaitu; the incident was forgotten, and time resumed its languid course.[34]

Her reproach only heightens his exquisite self-regard. The colonial relationship of their affair is sealed by it.

When he is absent for several months, he holds it to her credit that, though she could not resist returning from the country to the port, she had only one European lover. But throughout the affair she has suffered from consumption, and her cough gets worse.

After their parting Loti receives two pathetic letters from her, telling him of her sadness and her faithfulness to him. But shortly after the second, he hears of her subsequent life: she had returned to Pape'ete and taken up with a succession of lovers. Later he hears that she had died at eighteen, destitute, emaciated by consumption, and addicted to brandy. It is a touching story of a Cressida who broke nobody's heart but her own, and of a young officer of a master race who had claimed *droit de seigneur* for the best year of her life.

The central relationship in Robert Louis Stevenson's best-known story of the South Pacific is between a trader and his part-Polynesian wife. The story I mean is 'The Beach at Falesa'. The wife of Wiltshire, the trader, herself the daughter of a trader and woman from another island, is conscious of being half-caste and has rejected the attentions of a full Polynesian, but, not being native to the island, she is disliked by the local people. Wiltshire has little respect for her, and is content to be married with a hoax certificate, which she treasures as a security or badge of respectability. But when he finds that she blames herself for the ostracism he suffers from the local people, when he sees her sob like a child, he is touched. The scene is unsubtle, perhaps not quite so revealing as the passage from Loti. ' "Uma," I said. "I would rather have you than all the copra in the South Seas", which was a very big expression, and the strangest thing was that I meant it.'[35]

She tells him that she loves him because — as he knows to be untrue — he is not ashamed of her. The mutual confession of attitudes that they had not been aware of sets off a revolution in his own attitude to her, so that in the end he is proud of his part-Polynesian children, and doesn't object to the prospect of his daughter marrying a Polynesian. She remains the same, a contented female Friday. However, there are literary objections one can make. The very distance between the two, the sparseness of their exchanges in the unsatisfactory lingua franca in which they speak to each other, preclude any subtlety or profundity or any kind of discovery in their relationship. It is all rather simple and obvious. The narrative interest in the story comes from the suspense created by the intrigue and rivalry among expatriate traders. The local people are passive and malign, their prejudices and superstition manipulated by the villainous rival trader.

There is in fact not much in Stevenson's Pacific writing that is of high literary order. Most of his best work had been written before he came to the Pacific. The three novels he wrote in collaboration with his stepson Lloyd Osbourne are adventure stories about white men, for which the Pacific is little more than a background stretch of ocean. The most interesting of his books is *In the South Seas*, a collection of yachtsman's observations originally written for a New York weekly. Both the editor and Stevenson's agent were disappointed with them, because they were not the informal diary in the form of letters that they had expected. Stevenson was disappointed with them, for a different reason. He had envisaged something more ambitious: '*the* big book on the South Seas'. His description of the material of the book suggests that what he put most value on was the impact of a variety of experience unfamiliar to his readership. He wrote to Sidney Colvin: 'At least, nobody has had such stuff; such wild stories, such beautiful scenes, such singular intimacies, such manners and traditions, so incredible a mixture of the beautiful and horrible, the savage and civilised.'[36]

The instalments as he wrote them fall between the two aims of casual, spontaneous journalistic impressions, and reflective essays on the Pacific as he saw it, in a state of transition between past savagery and modern domestication. Later he told Colvin that the letters were no more than a quarry for his planned 'big book on the South Seas'.[37]

Discovering correspondences between Pacific and European institutions was one of Stevenson's pleasures and this motive seems to have inspired his two other stories in *Island Nights' Entertainments*. The idea of 'The Bottle Imp' he took from an English melodrama of 1828. Whether he knew it or not, the plot is from a German folk-tale, and he perceived in it certain likenesses in ingenuity to Hawaiian folk-tales. He set it in Hawaii and had it translated into Samoan. 'The Isle of Voices' he appears to have taken from a Tuamotuan legend told him by the French Vice-Resident on Fakarava; but as he works it up, it is — I think — a mystifying story, neither allegory or satisfying myth; something of an ingenious attempt to convert a folk-tale into a teasing ghost story — I am not sure whether it is playful or slightly pretentious.

It is not possible in the time left to do justice to the copious writing of Louis Becke, the Australian who had spent nearly twenty years of his early life as a trader, and visited most of the islands of the Pacific, whose tales have been regarded highly by 'old Pacific hands' of the earlier years of this century, not I imagine for good critical reasons, but for the recognizable authenticity of his background and subject matter. The variety of experience that Stevenson was excited by, Becke was familiar with: 'such wild stories . . . such singular intimacies . . . so incredible a mixture of the beautiful and the horrible, the savage and the civilised'. There was hardly a variety of European commercial activity in the Pacific that Becke wasn't knowledgeable about — the work of lonely copra traders, the arduous life of captains and supercargoes of trading vessels, and the harshness of the labour trade.

He was encouraged at first by the editor by the Sydney *Bulletin*, J. F. Archibald, to write the earliest of his short tales in the laconic, unromantic style that the *Bulletin* favoured. It is in fact sentimental, and often seems morally indifferent to the point of cynicism. The point of view is from the beach, or the trading ship — meeting places of decivilized Europeans and Pacific Islanders who are either displaced and somewhat demoralized individuals, or a rather undifferentiated mass of local people, sometimes sullen or superstitious, often unpredictable. The European may be a lonely trader, often alcoholic and without conscience, or perhaps touchingly devoted in a simple way to a 'native wife' — I put the expression in quotation marks because usually the trader's wife is not a native of the island and is for that reason disliked. The 'native' woman has passion and infidelity in her blood, and is capable of murder of a rival or of the husband who stands in the way of new love. There is something bleak about Becke's moral world, a shrug at injustice and cruelty. There is, at least in some of the tales, a peculiarly unfocused quality about the literary effects Becke is aiming for. This is reflected in the technique of shifting the point of view, either the point of view in time or in the identity of the informant, with a row of dots every few paragraphs. It is reflected too in the uncertainty of effect of the ending.

In 'The Last Cruise of John Maudsley, Recruiter' for example, published in 1899, Maudsley is the mate of a vessel with a hold full of labourers recruited from the New Hebrides. The ship is becalmed ten miles from land. There is not enough air in the hold and there is measles among the labourers. Maudsley recommends that they be put ashore at Alofi, uninhabited, though planted, and medical attention be sought at Futuna, a few miles away. But the men in the hold are not aware of his plan and revolt. Many of them are shot and, getting them back to the hold, Maudsley is tomahawked. The focus at the end dwells on a number of sentimental circumstances peculiar to Maudsley, and to the second mate who had died of fever. Maudsley feels guilty because he had persuaded that man to make the cruise, and since he is dying he leaves his money from this cruise to the captain to pass on to the second mate's fiancée. But there is no overt sympathy for the labourers in the hold except in Maudsley's concern for them. It is possible to make more than one interpretation of this story: either the cynical moral that Maudsley's humaneness was pity wasted in a tough world; or that his humaneness in a callous trade was a self-deception, and he got what he could expect for being part of that trade. But if the implication is the second of these, one would expect more sympathy for the desperate people in the hold, and less distraction about the white sweetheart back home. In fact the most apparent interpretation is the trite and myopic one that it was undeserved bad luck for Maudsley that this trip had gone so badly, but he met his luck with commendable stoicism and generosity. The author's sympathy seems to be analogous to the attitude by which the killed labourers are thrown overboard and their blood washed off the deck, while the body of a white crewman is carried aft and laid beside the second mate's, to await the attention of the Catholic priest at Futuna.[38]

In another tale a fat German planter has a part-Samoan girl educated at a convent in preparation for her marriage to him. But the day before the wedding a handsome part-Manihikian boatswain coaxes her to join him on a trading voyage. He treats her roughly, and she likes him all the better for it; and in time he drops her for someone else. The planter writes asking her to come back to him, but she says he hasn't sent enough money and she wants to wait for an American naval ship due in Apia. The title of the story is ''Tis in the Blood'. In this story there are several issues on which the narrator is non-committal; but the impression is that the planter is mocked for his naivety, Vaega's fickleness is to be expected, and Allan the boatswain is wryly admired for his success.

There is something parochial about this: a yarn for the knowing about people known, or stereotypes known, to impress the stranger who is treated as an initiate. The values of the old hands are not questioned, or contradictions explored.

The inhabitants of islands are often presented as very cruel. In one tale set in the Marquesas, a former convict O'Shea is tired of a part-Tahitian wife Sera who hates him for his cruelty. When he buys the half-caste daughter of a trader as a new wife, Sera stabs her. It is the local people, in O'Shea's presence, who execute a viciously cruel punishment; she is tied across the bilge of a boat and whipped with the tail of a stingray. O'Shea has further punishment in mind but the story ends sentimentally with her death cheating him of that satisfaction. To me one of the incredibilities of the story is the process of justice, only hinted at but apparently chiefly and pre-colonial, which is apparently swayed by fear of O'Shea and by the women's dislike of one for whom they knew to be 'better and more pure than themselves'; and another incredibility is the 'two pairs of small eager brown hands' that fix her to the keel of the boat before her punishment. Sera dies without giving sign of her agony, and on that obtuse impression of stiff upper lip the story ends.

In a story set on Majuro in the Marshall Islands a trader who marries a chief's daughter Le-jennabon discovers that she has made an assignation with a visiting young chief from a nearby island. Outside a boy is singing a mocking song, 'Marriage hides the tricks of lovers'. When the trader decides what he will do, he slides a rifle inside his pyjamas and his cook grins — 'the cook-hag' she is called. She follows him and when he shoots the lover, the cook hands him a knife and holds the lover's head back by his long hair to enable him to cut off his head. The trader punishes his wife by making her walk ahead of him through the village with her lover's head in her hands singing 'Marriage hides the tricks of lovers'. It is a no more than a neatly symmetrical tale of revenge. The story ends with the trader's comment that it has made his wife faithful and raised him in the esteem of the local people. That is probably an ironic coda. But the local people have been belittled. If the point is that some traders are savages, the local people are not much better.

A last example is the story of a New Zealand trader who is wrecked on Vahitahi, one of the Tuamotus, and marries a local girl Luita, who is jealous when he speaks of his wife at home. His sister comes looking for him while he is away on a trading voyage, and Luita leaves for another island where she pines from jealousy. The trader follows her there to find her dying and shoots himself. It is a sentimental story of well-meant misunderstanding and touching jealousy in which the pathos depends on a woman's subjection.[39]

In these stories the violence is gratuitous, and seldom has other consequence than further violence or enforced obedience. Some stories turn into short melodramas. There is a lack of subtlety or definition in relationships. There is a strong element of fortuitousness. When one compares Becke's Pacific say with Conrad's Congo in *The Heart of Darkness*, one sees that there is no sense of the sinister engine of imperialism operating from a distance, only of unpredictability, against which a rifle is an advisable safeguard. There is a notable lack of criticism or even of the desire for any other kind of world than this one free from the restraints of home society, free from the operation of conscience. The more immediate aim is that of a teller of yarns — to impress the tame homebody with the wild experience accessible only a few years earlier and close to home.

I don't propose to follow into the twentieth century the writers who have set their fiction in the Pacific, no less numerous than their predecessors in the eighteenth and nineteenth. We have seen that even in the most gifted, their perception of Pacific cultures has been limited or distracted by European philosophical preoccupations or by desires that originated in European culture. The most interesting has been the writing with the least preconception — that of the eighteenth-century navigators and the early nineteenth-century beachcombers; and the writing of greatest accomplishment that of Melville. On the whole it has not been innovative in technique.

It is to be expected that the view from inside the Pacific communities would be different, and the access to traditions and literary models different. Nevertheless I doubt if anyone in the west twenty years ago could have predicted the vigorous growth of Pacific-born literature or the direction it has taken.

I want to end by throwing out a number of suggestions. The spirit of ridicule and playfulness that was evident in the dramatic performances of the arioi, with which I opened the first of these lectures, appears in some stories by the Tongan writer Epeli Hau'ofa and in some satirical chapters by Albert Wendt. In Wendt's novels one sees that if sanctuaries have been rifled, it was the souls of the people that were robbed of old securities, and new ones slipped in. Christian rectitude is a central pillar of what the traditionalist characters in *Leaves of the Banyan Tree* call *fa'a-Samoa*, the Samoan way of doing things: and the loudest of those who profess it, are shown as seekers of power and honour in the terms of western commercial enterprise. Yet there are elements in the behaviour of these traditionalists that belong to an older tradition — the strong ties of family, the rivalry of clans for prestige and power, the violence, and the obedience of the women. Those elderly leaders who have always been sceptical of Christianity are vague and unsure when they look for the ancient securities that have disappeared.

There is a statement by a character in a play by Jo Nacola that though he likes to talk Fijian, there are some things he cannot talk about in

Fijian because the people who speak Fijian best do not talk about them. So there are some thoughts he can only express in English.[40] In a comparable way, Albert Wendt goes to European ideas for a solution, to the writing of Camus for his thoughts on the void left by the loss of faith in Christianity; and to Camus's ideas on myth to enable him to undertake a bold recreation of traditional myth. Those who see furthest have attributes of the trickster hero of Polynesian myth. The new culture-hero, who has some of the mythical attributes of a god or something more than man, who might restore mana and tapu to the sanctuary, is tried out in the character Galupo, the apparently amoral restorer in *Leaves of the Banyan Tree*, a man widely read in western literature and philosophy.

There are of course other recent writers in English, from Papua-New Guinea, the Solomon Islands, Vanuatu, Fiji, Niue, Kiripati, and the Cook Islands. In editing an anthology of this writing, Albert Wendt recognizes that the common theme of anti-colonialism is a temporary thing, and he recognizes an incidentally liberating effect of colonialism, which having destroyed the traditional styles of art, made possible the individual styles of the modern artist.[41] There is the rich source of oral tradition, of which only a few European writers like Stevenson and some later missionaries made use, using rather stale western models for their form. If the people of the newly independent island states are able to support a number of writers and artists, the view from the villages and the towns is likely to contain further surprises.

REFERENCES
1 FALL FROM GRACE
1. The fullest and most recent consideration of the *arioi* is in Douglas L. Oliver, *Ancient Tahitian Society*, 3 v., Honolulu and Canberra, 1974, v.3, pp.913-64.
2. James Cook, *The Journals of Captain James Cook on His Voyage of Discovery...*, v.2, *The Voyage of the Resolution and Adventure, 1772-1775*, J. C. Beaglehole (ed.), Cambridge, 1961, pp.223-4.
3. Op. cit., v.2, pp.413, 840.
4. Johann Reinhold Forster, *Observations made during a Voyage Round the World on Physical Geography, Natural History and Ethic Philosophy...*, London, 1778, pp.473-5.
5. George (i.e. Johann Georg Adam) Forster, *A Voyage Round the World in His Britannic Majesty's Sloop Resolution, ... during the Years 1772, 3, 4 and 5*, 2 v., London, 1777, v.1, pp.364-5.
6. See my articles, 'European Intimidation and the Myth of Tahiti', *Journal of Pacific History*, v.5, 1969, pp.199-217, and 'The Reception of European Voyagers on Polynesian Islands 1568-1797', *Journal de la Société des Océanistes*, v.26, 1970, pp.121-54.
7. John Hawkesworth, *An Account of the Voyages ... in the Southern Hemisphere by Commodore Byron, Captain Wallis, Captain Carteret, and Captain Cook*, 3 v., London, 1773, v.2, p.197. Cf. *The Endeavour Journal of Joseph Banks 1768-1771*, ed. J. C. Beaglehole, v.1, pp.341-2; and James Cook, *Journals*, ed. J. C. Beaglehole, v.1, *The Voyage of the Endeavour 1768-1771*, p.121, also pp.ccciii-cv.
8. Nicolas Bricaire de la Dixmerie, *Le Sauvage de Taïti aux Français*, London and Paris, 1770.
9. Louis Antoine de Bougainville, *A Voyage Round the World ... 1766-1769*, translated by J. R. Forster, London, 1772; facsimile, Amsterdam and New York, 1967, pp.257-8 (cf. *Voyage autour du Monde Par La Frégate "La Boudeuse" et la Flûte "L'Etoile"*, Cercle du Bibliophile, [Levallois-Perret], 1969, p.146).
10. P. P. Gudin de la Brenellerie, *Aux Manes de Louis XV et des Grands Hommes qui ont vecu sous son regne*, Deux Ponts, 1776, pp.113-14.
11. See my essay, 'Hawkesworth's Alterations', *Journal of Pacific History*, v.7, 1972, pp.45-72.
12. Bernard Smith, *European Vision in the South Pacific 1768-1850*, Oxford, 1960; E. H. McCormick, *Omai, Pacific Envoy*, Auckland and Oxford, 1977, ch.12; Colin Roderick, 'Sir Joseph Banks, Queen Oberea and the Satirists', in *Captain James Cook: Image and Impact*, ed. Walter Veit, Melbourne, 1972.
13. *The Works of Peter Pindar, Esq.*, 4 v., London, 1816, v.1, p.464.
14. *An Historic Epistle from Omiah, to the Queen of Otaheite: being his remarks on the English Nation*, London, 1775, p.43.
15. *The Anti-Jacobin; or Weekly Examiner*, 2 April 1789, p.166.
16. *The Life and Correspondence of the Late Robert Southey*, ed. C. C. Southey, 6 v., London 1849-50, v.1, p.119.
17. J. G. A. Forster, *A Voyage Round the World*, v.2, p.122.

18. J. G. A. Forster, op. cit., v.1, p.303.
19. J. R. Forster, *Observations Made During a Voyage*...., p.304.
20. J. G. A. Forster, op. cit., v.2, p.111.
21. Henry Adams, *Tahiti*, Memoirs of Arii Taimai, Paris, 1901 (reprint, New York, 1947), pp.41-46, 57-61.
22. [Rev. Gerald Fitzgerald], *The Injured Islanders; or, the Influence of Art upon the Happiness of Nature*, London, 1779, p.7.
23. Mme de Monbart, *Lettres Taitiennes*, Paris, (n.d.).
24. N. Bricaire de la Dixmerie, *Le Sauvage de Taïti*....; Voltaire, 'Les Oreilles du Comte de Chesterfield et le Chapelain Goudman', 1775, in v.60 of *Oeuvres Complètes*, Paris, 1826; [Taitbout], *Essai sur l'Isle d'Otahiti*..., Avignon and Paris, 1779.
25. [J. C. Poncelin de la Roche-Tilhac], *Histoire Philosophique de la Naissance, du Progrès et de la Décadence d'un Grand Royaume ou Révolutions de Taïti*..., Paris, 1784.
26. [G. A. R. Baston], *Narrations d'Omaï*, Rouen and Paris, 1790.
27. Denis Diderot, 'Supplément au Voyage de Bougainville' (written 1772, published 1796) in *Selected Philosophical Writings*, ed. J. Lough (Cambridge, 1953), p.167, or v.10, *Oeuvres Complètes*, Paris, 1971, p.205.
28. Anna Seward, *Elegy on Captain Cook*..., London, 1780.
29. J. F. Arnould-Mussot, *La Mort du Capitaine Cook*..., Paris, 1788; *The Death of Captain Cook*; grand-serious-pantomimic ballet in three parts..., London, 1789.
30. Charlotte Beverley, 'Verses on the Death of Capt. Cook...' in *Poems on Miscellaneous Subjects*, Hull, 1792.
31. [James Wilson], *A Missionary Voyage to the Southern Pacific Ocean, performed in the years 1796, 1797, 1798, in the Ship Duff, commanded by Capt. James Wilson, compiled from Journals of the Officers and the Missionaries*...., London, 1799, pp.385, 384.
32. Letter to Grosvenor Charles Bedford, 2 February 1793, in *New Letters of Robert Southey*, ed. Kenneth Curry, New York, 1965, v.1, p.19.
33. 'Transactions of the Missionary Society', *Annual Review*, 3, 1804, pp.621-34.
34. Letter to John Rickman, 23 December 1803, in *Life and Correspondence*, v.2, p.243; *Quarterly Review*, v.2, 1809, p.45.
35. *Quarterly Review*, v.2, 1809, p.45.
36. Letter to Rickman, cited in note 34.
37. *Quarterly Review*, v.43, 1830, p.54.

2 RESCUE AND CAPTIVITY

1. W. M. Praed, *Australasia*..., Cambridge, 1823, pp.12-13.
2. Robert Grant, *Kapiolani, with Other Poems*, London, 1848.
3. James Montgomery to George Bennet, 11 June 1829, in George Bennet, [Poems and a Letter addressed to George Bennet], printed by J. M. Showell, Birmingham, n.d., pp.6-7.
4. James Greenwood, *Curiosities of Savage Life*, 2 v., 3rd ed., London, 1865.
5. James Montgomery, 'The Pelican Island', in *The Poetical Works of James Montgomery*, London, 3 v., 1836, v.2, pp.57, 61.
6. Samuel Lucas, *The Sandwich Islands, a Prize Poem*, Oxford, 1841, p.12.
7. Sarah Ellis, *The Island Queen: a Poem*, London, 1846, pp.46,85.
8. (George Macfarren and T. L. Prest], *The String of Pearls; or The Barber of Fleet Street*, London, 1840, p.17.
9. 'The King of the Cannibal Islands, A Popular Comic Song' written by Mr A. W. Humphreys ... London, n.d. [?1830]; also included in B. Williams's *Collection of the*

most favorite Comic Songs, London, [1864]; *Harlequin and Ponoowingkeewang*... New Xmas Pantomime, 1845, Brit.Mus.Add. MSS 42990; *The New Christmas Pantomine, Poonoowingkeewang or Harlequin Hokey Pokey and the King of the Canibal Islands*, Brit. Mus. Add. MSS 43038A.

10. Harriet Martineau, *Dawn Island, a Tale*, Manchester, 1845, p.16.
11. Frederick Chamier, *Jack Adams, The Mutineer*, 3 v., London, 1838, v.1, p.76.
12. F. B. Miller, *Tales of Travel*, London, 1833, pp.142-3.
12a. *The Tahitians; or, Christianity in the South Seas. A Dramatic Poem*, Cheltenham, 1838; John Dunlop, *The South Sea Islanders: A Christian Tale...*, London, 1841.
13. Niel Gunson in *Messengers of Grace*, (Melbourne, 1978) on p.183 mentions 'Mahine'; Joseph Waterhouse, *Vah-ta-ah, the Feejeean Princess*, London, 1857, p.[12]. *most favorite Comic Songs*, London, [1864]; *Harlequin and Ponoowingkeewang*... New Xmas Pantomime, 1845, Brit.Mus.Add. MSS 42990; *The New Christmas Pantomine, Poonoowingkeewang or Harlequin Hokey Pokey and the King of the Canibal Islands*, Brit. Mus. Add. MSS 43038A.
10. Harriet Martineau, *Dawn Island, a Tale*, Manchester, 1845, p.16.
11. Frederick Chamier, *Jack Adams, The Mutineer*, 3 v., London, 1838, v.1, p.76.
12. F. B. Miller, *Tales of Travel*, London, 1833, pp.142-3.
13. Niel Gunson in *Messengers of Grace*, (Melbourne, 1978) on p.183 mentions 'Mahine'; Joseph Waterhouse, *Vah-ta-ah, the Feejeean Princess*, London, 1857, p.[12].
14. Jesse Carey, *The Kings of the Reefs*, Melbourne, 1891.
15. [Samuel Tamatoa Williams], *Pomare, Queen of Tahiti*, a Poem, London, 1847, pp.9,11.
16. Sarah Ellis, *The Island Queen, A Poem*, London, 1846, p.34.
17. Op. cit., pp.40, 66.
18. Mrs Favell Lee Mortimer, *The Night of Toil*... (1838), 2nd ed., London, 1844, p.vii.
19. Charles Wall, *The Orphan's Isle*, London, 1838, p.223.
20. N. W. Fiske, *Tuwarri, a Story of the Coral Isles*, Boston, 1848, pp.25-26.
21. John Martin, *An Account of the Natives of the Tonga Islands*, 2 v., London, 1817, v.1, pp.301-2.
22. Op. cit., v.2, pp.42, 52.
23. See Robert B. Nicholson, *The Pitcairners*, Sydney, 1965; H. E. Maude, 'In Search of a Home', in *Of Islands and Men*, Melbourne, 1968.
24. *Quarterly Review*, v.13, (1815), p.383.
25. Mary Russell Mitford, *Christina, The Maid of the South Seas; a Poem*, London, 1811.
26. George Gordon Noel Byron, *The Island, or Christian and his Comrades*, London, 1823, Canto II, lines 67-70.
27. *The Story of Aleck, of Pitcairn's Island*, Amherst, Mass., 1829; [Charles S. Sargent], *The Life of Alexander Smith, Captain of the Island of Pitcairn*, Boston, 1819.
28. Frederick Chamier, *Jack Adams, the Mutineer*, London, 1838, p.134.
29. Harriet Martineau, *Dawn Island, A Tale*, Manchester, 1845, pp.88, 93-94; William Ellis, *Polynesian Researches*, 4 v., London, 1831, v.2, p.397.
30. [Timothy Flint], *The Life and Adventures of Arthur Clenning*, Philadelphia, 1828.
31. James Fenimore Cooper, *The Crater, or Vulcan's Peak*, New York, 1847.
32. Benjamin Morrell, *A Narrative of Four Voyages... from the Year 1822 to 1831*, New York, 1832; Rupert T. Gould, *Enigmas*, London, 1929, p.255, n.
33. Henry R. Stommel, ' "The Biggest Liar of the Pacific," Capt. Benjamin Morrell, Jr.', unpublished paper accepted for the *Mariners' Mirror*, written in 1981.
34. See newspaper report in the *Baltimore Patriot Mercantile Advertiser*, 29 November 1831, cited in *American Activities in the Central Pacific 1790-1870*, ed. R. Gerard Ward, 7 v., Ridgewood, New Jersey, 1967, v.7, pp.239-56; Henry Bergh, 'Biographical Sketch of Christian Bergh', *New York Times*, 18 March 1888, p.11; John Keeler, *The South Sea Islanders*... New York, 1831, p.[4].

35. John Keeler, Journal of a Voyage to the South Seas June 24th 1828 -, Log 339, G. W. Blunt White Library, Mystic, Connecticut, entry for 17 May 1830.
36. Benjamin Morrell, *Narrative of Four Voyages*, pp.393, 436.
37. Op. cit., pp.403-13.
38. Andrew Cheyne, *A Description of Islands in the Western Pacific Ocean* . . . London, 1852, pp.126-7; Dorothy Shineberg (ed.), *The Trading Voyages of Andrew Cheyne 1841-1844*, Canberra, 1971, p.24; Alexander G. Findlay, *A Directory for the Navigation of the Pacific Ocean*, 2 v., London, 1851, pp.1088-9; second edition (North Pacific), [1870], p.758.
39. See Francis X. Hezel, 'The Beginnings of Foreign Contact with Truk', *Journal of Pacific History*, v.8, 1973, pp.51-73.
40. Morrell, op. cit., pp.422-34, in particular pp.427, 432-3.
41. William Skiddy, The Ups and Downs of a Sea Life, 1805-1839, Misc. MSS, v.157, 158, G. W. Blunt White Library, Mystic, Connecticut. For Woodworth's play see *New York Mirror*, 16 March 1833, p.295; O. S. Coad, 'The Plays of Samuel Woodworth', *Sewanee Review*, v.27, 1919, pp.171-2.
42. Kendall B. Taft, 'Samuel Woodworth', doctoral thesis, University of Chicago, 1936, p.161; T. J. Jacobs (see Note 45), pp.16, 363.
43. Roy Harvey Pearce, 'The Significances of the Captivity Narrative', *American Literature*, v.19, 1947-8, pp.1-20; also Phillips D. Carleton, 'The Indian Captivity', *American Literature*, v.15, 1943, pp.169-80.
44. Abby Jane Morrell, *Narrative of a Voyage*. . . New York, 1833; *Voyages and Adventures of Jack Halliard with Captain Morrell*, Boston, 1833; Edgar Allan Poe, *The Narrative of Arthur Gordon Pym of Nantucket* (1837), Penguin, Harmondsworth, 1975, pp.202-4 (cf. B. Morrell, op. cit. pp.401-2); Morton M. Sealts, *Melville's Reading*, Madison, Wisconsin, 1966, pp.71, 81.
45. Thomas Jefferson Jacobs, *Scenes, Incidents and Adventures in the Pacific Ocean*. . . , New York, 1844.
46. Charles W. Denison, *Old Slade, or Fifteen Years' Adventures of a Sailor*, Boston, 1844; William Torrey, *Torrey's Narrative*, Boston, 1848; Louis A. Baker, *Harry Martingale, or, Adventures of a Whaleman in the Pacific Ocean*, Boston, 1848; [Joseph C. Hart], *Miriam Coffin, or the Whale-Fishermen*, New York, 1834.
47. *The Modern Crusoe; or, the King of the Cannibals of the Marquesas Islands*, London, 1869. First published in *The Weekly Budget* (London), 22 May-14 August 1869.
48. *Newspaper Press Directory*, 1869.
49. [James F. Bowman], *The Island Home, or the Young Castaways*, edited by Christopher Romaunt, Boston, 1851, 1852, 1864; London, 1852; Richard Archer, *The Island Home, or the Adventures of Six Young Crusoes*, London, 1853, 1873; [Anon.], *The Island Home, or the Young Castaways*, London, 1877, 1892; [E. M. Lucett], *Rovings in the Pacific from 1837 to 1849.* . . . By a Merchant Long Resident at Tahiti, 2v., London, 1851, v.1, pp.248-54.
50. Bowman, op. cit., London, 1873 edition, pp.378, 379.
51. Eric Quayle, *The Collector's Book of Boys' Stories*, London, 1973, p.49. The popularized account was J. S. Jenkins, *Recent Exploring Expeditions to the Pacific and the South Seas*, New York, 1852; London, 1853.
52. Eric Quayle, *Ballantyne the Brave*, London, 1967, pp.161-5.
53. W. H. G. Kingston, *A Lecture on Colonization*, London, 1849, p.6.
54. *Kingston's Magazine*, v.4, p.201, cited in M. R. Kingsford, *The Life . . . of W. H. G. Kingston*, Toronto, 1947, pp.181-2.
55. *Boys' Own Paper*, v.2, 2 August 1880, p.796.
56. Cited in Kingsford, op. cit.
57. R. M. Ballantyne, *The Coral Island*, London, 1858, p.224 (ch.19).
58. Quayle, op. cit., p.163; Ballantyne, op. cit., pp.242-3 (ch.20).

59. Op. cit., p.279 (ch.23).
60. Op. cit., p.371 (ch.30).
61. Op. cit., pp.414, 415 (ch.33).
62. Op. cit., p.232 (ch.19).
63. R. M. Ballantyne, *Gascoyne the Sandalwood Trader*, London, 1864, p.405 (ch.31).
64. R. M. Ballantyne, *Tales of Adventure by Flood, Field and Mountain*, London, 1874, p.122.
65. W. H. G. Kingston, *Mary Liddiard; or, The Missionary's Daughter* (1873); *Little Ben Hadden, or, Do Right, Whatever Comes of It* (1870, 1880, 1883, 1907); *Round the World, a Tale for Boys* (1859); *Peter Trawl; or The Adventures of a Whaler* (1881, 1909); *Old Jack, a Tale for Boys* (1860, 1871, 1899, 1911, and in *Boys' Sea Story Omnibus*, Collins, London, 1934).
66. Niel Gunson, *Messengers of Grace*, Melbourne, 1978, p.273.
67. Kingston, *Old Jack*, 1871 edition, pp.479-83, 497-8.

3 VIEWS FROM THE BEACH

1. G. H. von Langsdorff, *Voyages and Travels in various Parts of the World During the Years 1803, 1804, 1805, 1806 and 1807* . . . , London, 1813.
2. Robert Ker Porter, *Travelling Sketches in Russia and Sweden, During the Years 1805, 1806, 1807, 1808*, 2 v., London, 1809, v.2, pp.40-50; Greg Dening, *Islands and Beaches*, Carlton, Victoria, 1980.
3. Jane Porter, 'The South Sea Chief', *Sydney Gazette*, 10 September 1829.
4. Edited, with introduction by Jennifer Terrell, 'Joseph Kabris and his notes on the Marquesas', *Journal of Pacific History*, v.17, (1982), pp.101-12.
5. H. E. Maude, 'Beachcombers and Castaways' in *Of Islands and Men*, Melbourne, 1968, p.169.
6. 'Locksley Hall', lines 157-84, *The Poems of Tennyson*, ed. Christopher Ricks, London, 1969, pp.697-9.
7. Herman Melville, *Typee*, Evanston, 1968, pp.70-71.
8. *The Marquesan Journal of Edward Robarts 1797-1824*, ed. Greg Dening, Canberra, 1974, pp.53-54.
9. Robarts, op. cit., pp.257-9.
10. Robarts, op. cit., p.160.
11. John Martin, *An Account of the Natives of the Tonga Islands*, 2 v., London, 1817, v.1, p.91.
12. Denis Joroyal McCulloch in John Martin, *Tonga Islands* (4th edition), Neiafu, Tonga, 1981, p.12.
13. Martin, op. cit., (1817), v.2, pp.53-55.
14. Sarah Ellis, *The Island Queen*, London, 1846, p.107.
15. [William Diaper], *Cannibal Jack: The True Autobiography of a White Man in the South Seas* by William Diapea. . . , London, 1928, sections 16 and 17.
16. See 'Textual Record' by the editors (Harrison Hayford, Hershel Parker, G. Thomas Tanselle) in the Northwestern University edition of *Typee*, Evanston, 1968, pp.303-59.
17. C. S. Stewart, *A Visit to the South Seas*. . . , 2 v., New York, 1831, v.1, p.295.
18. David Porter, *Journal of a Cruise* . . . *to the Pacific Ocean*, 2nd ed., 2 v., New York, 1822 (reprinted New York, 1970), v.2, chs.13, 14, 15.
19. Melville, *Typee*, 1968, p.201.
20. Robarts, *Marquesan Journal*, p.77.
21. Melville, *Typee*, p.177.
22. Louise K. Barnett, *The Ignoble Savage, American Literary Racism 1790-1890*, Westport, Connecticut, 1975.

23. Herman Melville, 'A Lecture on the South Seas' (1859) in *Melville's South Seas*, ed. A. Grove Day, New York, 1970, pp.273-9.
24. Sketch in [Great Britain. Admiralty, Naval Intelligence Division, Geographical Handbook Series:] *Pacific Islands*, 4 v., 1943-5 [ed. J. W. Davidson], v.2, *Eastern Pacific*, Fig.84 on p.287.
25. D. H. Lawrence, *Studies in Classic American Literature*, New York, 1964, pp.133, 134.
26. D. H. *Lawrence: A Composite Biography*, ed. Edward Nehls, 3 v., Madison, 1957-9, v.2, *1919-1925*, p.161; *The Collected Letters of D. H. Lawrence*, ed. Harry T. Moore, 2 v., London, 1962, v.2, p.713.
27. D. H. Lawrence, *Studies in Classic American Literature*, pp.136-7. See also Harry T. Moore, *The Intelligent Heart, The Story of D. H. Lawrence*, London, 1955.
28. D. H. Lawrence, *The Symbolic Meaning*, ed. Armin Arnold, [Arundel], 1962, p.222.
29. D. H. Lawrence, 'Indians and an Englishman' (written autumn 1922, published in *The Dial*, February 1923), in *Selected Essays*, Harmondsworth, 1950, p.197.
30. Benjamin Morrell, *A Narrative of Four Voyages*, New York, 1832, pp.390, 424-5.
31. Dora Hort, *Hena; or, Life in Tahiti*, 2 v., London, 1866, v.1, pp.124, 34, 126, 154.
32. Dora Hort, *Tiari: a Tahitian Romance*, London, 1893, p.300.
33. Pierre Loti [i.e. Julien Viaud], *The Marriage of Loti*, tr. Wright and Eleanor Frierson, Honolulu, 1976, pp.112, 163.
34. Loti, op. cit., p.115.
35. R. L. Stevenson, *The Complete Short Stories of Robert Louis Stevenson*, ed. Charles Neider, Garden City, New York, 1969, p.606.
36. R. L. Stevenson, *Letters*, 4 v., (The Skerryvore Edition), London, 1926, v.3, p.158.
37. Stevenson, *Letters*, v.3, pp.291, 199.
38. Louis Becke, 'The Last Cruise of John Maudsley, Recruiter', in Lala Fisher (ed.), *By Creek and Gully . . .* , London, 1899.
39. 'The Revenge of Macy O'Shea', 'The Methodical Mr Burr of Majuru', and 'Brantley of Vahitahi' were first collected in Becke's first book of stories *By Reef and Palm*, London, 1894; latest edition, Sydney, 1955.
40. Jo Nacola, 'I Native No More', in *I Native No More*, Suva, 1976, p.37.
41. Albert Wendt (ed.), *Lali, A Pacific Anthology*, Auckland, 1980, pp.xiii-xix.

INDEX

A Directory for Navigation, Alexander G. Findlay, 45, 85
A Missionary Voyage to the Southern Pacific Ocean, [James Wilson], 27–28
Adams, John, 39, 40, 41
Afareaitu (Moʻorea), 75
Ahutoru, 15
Aimata (Pomare, later Tahitian queen), 35
Alofi, 78
American Indians, 20, 46–47
Amherst, Massachusetts, 37
Anderson, C. R., 66
'Angatan' (Angatau), 51, 56, 57
Antarctic, 44–46
Anti-Jacobin, 19, 71
Archibald, J. F., 78
arioi, 12, 17, 24, 40, 54
Arthur Clenning, Timothy Flint, 41–42

Baker, Louis A., 49, 86
Ballantyne, R. M., 52–56, 86
Banks, Joseph, 16
Barrow, John, 39
Baston, G. A. R., 23, 24, 84
Baxter, Archibald, 11
Baxter, James K., 11
Baxter, Millicent, 11
Beadle and Adams, 49, 58
Becke, Louis, 66, 77–81, 88
Bembo, 70
Bennet, George, 30–31, 84
Bergh, Christian, 45, 85
Beverley, Charlotte, 27, 84
Bougainville, Louis Antoine de, 14, 15, 37–38, 83
Bounty, mutiny, 39–41
Bowery Theatre, New York, 46
Bowman, James, 50, 56
Boy's Own Paper, 52
Brenellerie, Gudin de la, 15, 83

Bricaire de la Dixmerie, N., 23, 84
Brown, John Macmillan, 11
Buka, 43
Bulletin (Sydney), 78
Bunyip Land, George Manville Fenn, 57
Byron, George Gordon Noel, 19, 38, 40, 63, 67

Cabri, Jean, 59–60, 63, 67, 87
Cakobau, 35, 56
Camus, Albert, 82
cannibalism, 15, 27, 32–33, 49–50, 68
Canning, George, 19
captivity narrative, 46–47, 68–69
Carey, Jesse, 35, 85
Carlyle, Thomas, 36
Chamier, Frederick, 41, 85
Chartists, 52
Cheyne, Andrew, 45–46, 85
Christabel (*Christabel*, Samuel Taylor Coleridge), 36
Christian, Fletcher, 39–40
Coleridge, Samuel Taylor, 29, 36
Comptroller's Bay (Nukuhiva), 69
Conrad, Joseph, 80
Cook, James, 12, 26, 27, 45, 55
Cooper, H. Stonehewer, 71
Cooper, James Fenimore, 42, 46
Curiosities of Savage Life, James Greenwood, 31, 84
Curnow, Allen, 34n

Dawn Island, Harriet Martineau, 41, 85
Dening, Greg, 59, 68
Denison, Charles W. (*Old Slade*), 49
Diaper (Diapea), William, 65–66
Dickens, Charles, 34, 52
Diderot, Denis, 24, 84
Douglas, John, 18
Duff, 27–28, 37

Dunlop, John, 31-32, 34, 85

Ellis, Sarah Stickney, 32, 36-37, 63, 64-65, 85
Ellis, William, 27, 29, 32, 34, 35, 37, 41, 85
Erromanga, 48
Essai sur l'Isle d'Otahiti, Taitbout, 23, 84
Euilo (character), 50-51, 56

Fakarava, 77
Fangatau, 51
'Fayaway', 70
Fenn, George Manville, 57-58
Findlay, Alexander G., 45, 85
Fiji, 27-28, 65, 82
Finau, 65
Finau Fiji, 38
Finau Ulukalala, 38, 64
Fingal's Cave, 38
Fiske, N. W., Rev., 37, 85
Fitzgerald, Gerald, 21-22
Flint, Timothy, 41-42
Folger, Mayhew, Capt., 39, 40
Forster, George (Johann Georg Adam), 14, 19-21, 42, 54
Forster, Johann Reinhold, 12, 13, 19-21
Free Trade, 41
Forsythe, R. S., 66
Frere, John Hookham, 19
Freud, Sigmund, 38
Frierson, Wright and Eleanor (translators), 74, 88
Futuna, 78-79

Gascoyne, The Sandalwood Trader, R. M. Ballantyne, 52, 55-56, 86
Goldsmith, Oliver, 22, 30
Gothic novel, 59
Grant, Robert, 30, 84
Green, Toby, 61-62, 68-69
Greenwood, James, 31, 84
Gulliver Revived, R. E. Raspe, 42
Gunson, Niel, 57, 85, 87

Hala Api Api, 64
Harry Martingale, Louis A. Baker, 49, 86
Hauʻofa, Epeli, 81
Hawaii, 26, 32, 70, 77
Hawkesworth, John, 16, 17, 45, 49
Hazlitt, William, 19

Hena, Dora Hort, 73, 88
Hiva Oa, 50
hoax explorations, 47
Hoole, Elijah, 35
Hort, Dora, 73-74, 88
Howard, Leon, 69
Huahine, 12, 34
Humphreys, A. W., 33, 84-85

imaginary voyage as genre, 11
In the South Seas, R. L. Stevenson, 77
Indian captivity narrative, 46-47, 68-69
Indians, 20, 46-47
Island Nights' Entertainments, R. L. Stevenson, 77

Jacobs, Thomas Jefferson, 47-49, 50
Johnson, Samuel, 17

Kabris, Joseph, *see* Cabri, Jean
Kamchatka, 59
Kangaroo Island, 31
Kapiolani, 34
Keatonui, 62
Keeler, John, 43-46, 85
Kilauea, 30, 34
Kilinailau, 43, 44
King o' the Beach, George Manville Fenn, 58
Kingsmill islands (Kiripati), 49
Kingston, W. H. G., 52, 56-57, 86-87
Kiripati, 49, 82
Kusaie, 57

Langsdorff, G. H. von, 59, 67, 87
Lau, 65-66
Lawrence, D. H., 70-73
Le Sauvage de Taïti . . . , N. Bricaire de la Dixmerie, 23, 84
Leaves of the Banyan Tree, Albert Wendt, 81
Leeward Islands (Society Islands), 12-13, 34
Lettres Taitiennes, Mme de Monbart, 22-23
Litia, 65
Little Ben Hadden, W. H. G. Kingston, 56, 86
'Locksley Hall', Alfred Tennyson, 60-61, 87
Loti, Pierre (i.e. Julien Viaud), 74-76, 88
Lucas, Samuel, 32, 84

Lucett, E. M., 50-51
Luhan, Mabel Dodge, 71-72

McCormick, E. H., 18, 83
Macfarren, George, 33, 84
Madeline (*The Eve of St Agnes*, John Keats), 36
Ma'i (*see* Omai), 18
Majuro, 80
Manus, 48
Maré, 66
Margaret Oakley, 47
Mariner, William, 37-38, 49, 63-65, 67
Mark's Reef, Fenimore Cooper, 42
'Marnoo', 69
Marquesas, 27, 28, 49, 59-63, 79-80
Marryatt, Frederick, 46, 50
Marshall Islands, 80
Martin, John, 37-38, 63, 64, 85, 87
Martineau, Harriet, 33-34, 41, 85
Mary Liddiard, W. H. G. Kingston, 57, 86
Masterman Ready, Frederick Marryatt, 50
Maude, H. E., 60, 87
Mauritius, 47
Melville, Herman, 33, 34, 47, 49, 50, 57, 61-62, 66-72, 81, 87
Missionary Sketches, 31
Mitford, Mary Russell, 38, 39-40, 85
Monbart, Mme de, 22-23
'Monday', 43, 48
Montgomery, James, 31, 84
Mo'orea, 34, 75
Morrell, Abigail Jane, 43, 86
Morrell, Benjamin, 42-49, 50, 73, 85
Mortimer, Mrs Favell Lee, 35-36, 37, 85
'Mow Mow', 69
'Munchausen, Baron', 42
Murray, John, 66-67

Nacola, Jo, 81
Narage, 48
Narrations d'Omaï, G. A. R. Baston, 23, 24, 84
Narrative of Arthur Gordon Pym, Edgar Allan Poe, 47
Nat the Naturalist, George Manville Fenn, 57
Ndende, 48
New Britain, 43, 48
New Guinea, 48; hoax journeys into the interior, 47

New Hebrides, 27, 48, 78
New Ireland, 48, 63
Ninigo, 43
Niuafo'ou, 66
Nomoi, 73
Nukuhiva, 33, 39, 62, 63, 66-72
Nukuoro, 44

'Oberea', 14, 18, 21-22, 59
O'Brien, Edward, 71
Observations, J. R. Forster, 20, 21
Old Jack, W. H. G. Kingston, 57, 87
Old Slade, Charles W. Denison, 49, 86
Omai, 18, 19
Omoo, Herman Melville, 47, 66
Osbourne, Lloyd, 77

Pa'ati, 34
Pantomimes, 26-27, 33, 84, 84-85
Pape'ete, 71n, 73, 74, 76
Papua-New Guinea, 82
Pearce, Roy Harvey, 46, 86
Pele, 34
Peter Trawl, W. H. G. Kingston, 57, 87
Pitcairn, 39-41
Poe, Edgar Allan, 47
Polynesian Researches, William Ellis, 27, 29
Pomare (Tahitian chief), 34
Pomare (Tahitian queen), 35
Pomare, Samuel Tamatoa Williams, 35, 85
Poncelin de la Roche-Tilhac, J. C., 23, 84
Porter, David, 39, 67
Porter, Jane, 59-60, 87
Porter, Robert Ker, 59, 87
Praed, William Mackworth, 30, 84
Prest, T. L., 84
Purea (*see* Oberea), 14, 18, 21-22

Quarterly Review, 28-29, 71
Queequeg, 70

Ra'iatea, 12, 35
Rarahu, 'Pierre Loti', 74-76, 88
Rarotonga, 71, 71n
Révolutions de Taïti, J. C. Poncelin de la Roche-Tilhac, 23, 84
Robarts, Edward, 62-63, 67, 68, 87
Robertson, George, 16
Robinson Crusoe, Daniel Defoe, 25, 26
Roderick, Colin, 18, 83
Round the World, W. H. G. Kingston, 56-57, 87

Rousseau, Jean Jacques, 14, 15, 20
Rovings in the Pacific, E. M. Lucett, 50-51
Russell, M., Rev., 27

Samoa, 72, 81
Santa Cruz, 48
Sargent, Charles, 40
Scott, Walter, 64
Selkirk, Alexander, 25
Seward, Anna, 26, 84
Shaw, Leonard, 43, 47
Skiddaw, 30
Skiddy, William, Capt., 46
Smith, Alexander, 39, 40, 41
Smith, Bernard, 18, 83
Society Islands, 11-24, 25-26
Solomon Islands, 82
Southey, Robert, 19, 28-29, 37, 84
Staffa, 38
Stevenson, Robert Louis, 76-77, 78, 82, 88
Stewart, C. S., 67
Stickney, Sarah, 32
Stoddard, Charles Warren, 71
Stowe, Harriet Beecher, 42, 56
'Sunday', 43, 48
'Supplément au voyage de Bougainville', Denis Diderot, 24, 84
Swiss Family Robinson, J. D. Wyss, 50

Taha'a, 12
Tahiti, 11-24, 25-26, 63, 70, 71, 72, 73-76
Tahiti, or The Voice of Truth by A Lady, 35
Tahuata, 50, 62
Taipi clan, 39, 61-62
Taitbout, 23, 84
Tammany Hall, 43

Taos, New Mexico, 71
Tararo (character), 55
Tashtego, 70
Te Moana (Marquesan chief), 33
'Telum-by-by-Darco', 43, 48
Tennyson, Alfred, 60-61, 87
The Axe, Allen Curnow, 34n
'The Beach at Falesa', R. L. Stevenson, 76
'The Bottle Imp', R. L. Stevenson, 77
The Coral Island, R. M. Ballantyne, 52-55, 86
The Crater, Fenimore Cooper, 42
The Deserted Village, Oliver Goldsmith, 22

The Heart of Darkness, Joseph Conrad, 80-81
The Injured Islanders, Gerald Fitzgerald, 21-22
The Island, Lord Byron, 38-39
The Island Home, James F. Bowman, 50-51
'The Isle of Voices', R. L. Stevenson, 77
'The King of the Cannibal Islands', A. W. Humphreys, 33, 84-85
The Marriage of Loti, 'Pierre Loti', 74-76, 88
The Modern Crusoe, 47, 86
The Night of Toil, Mrs Favell Lee Mortimer, 37, 85
'The Pelican Island', James Montgomery, 31, 84
The Surprising Adventures of Baron Munchausen, 42
The Story of Aleck, anon., 40
The String of Pearls, George Macfarren and T. L. Priest, 32-33, 84
The Women of England, Sarah Stickney, 32
Tiari, Dora Hort, 74, 88
Tonga, 63-66, 85, 87
Torrey's Narrative, William Torrey, 49, 86
Truk, 45-46, 73
Tuamotu islands, 49, 63
Tyerman, Daniel, 30
Typee, Herman Melville, 47, 66-72
'Typees', 50, 57

Uncle Tom's Cabin, Harriet Beecher Stowe, 42, 56
United States Exploring Expedition, 27, 28

Vah-ta-ah, Joseph Waterhouse, 35, 85
Vahitahi, 80
Vaitahu, 50
Vanua Levu, 65
Vanuatu, 27, 48, 78, 88
Vava'u, 38, 66
Viaud, Julien, 74-76, 88
Voltaire, 23, 84
Voyages, John Hawkesworth, 16, 17

Wales, William, 12
Wall, Charles, 37, 85
Wallis, Samuel, 14, 16, 25, 49
Wallis island, 49
Walpole, Horace, 17
Waterhouse, Joseph, Rev., 35, 85

Wendt, Albert, 11, 81-82, 88
Wesley, Charles, 17
Wilkes, Charles, 27-28, 50
Williams, John, 27, 35
Williams, Samuel Tamatoa, 35-36

Wilson, James, 27-28, 37
Witu islands, 43, 48
Woodworth, Samuel, 46, 47
Wyss, J. D., 50